THE MECHANICS OF
GOD

*This is a **Garutman** book.*

Garutman began as a non-profit organisation aspiring to project Indian literature in translation.

   Garutman attempts to overcome the main hurdles in transcultural communication in order to project the core of Indian literature, staying as close to the original sources as possible. This is a sponsoring body for Indian literature in translation and shall be mainly concerned with establishing a community of translators and providing them with required assistance, arranging translation workshops, processing translations through a panel of editors, giving them required assistance, and arranging the publication and distribution of translated works.

THE MECHANICS OF
G·O·D

A THEORY ON THE TRANSITION OF SPECIES AND EVENTS

THOMAS EASLEY

ALLIED PUBLISHERS LIMITED
NEW DELHI BOMBAY CALCUTTA MADRAS NAGPUR
AHMEDABAD BANGALORE HYDERABAD LUCKNOW

ALLIED PUBLISHERS LIMITED

Regd. Off.: 15 J.N. Heredia Marg, Ballard Estate, Bombay 400038
Prarthna Flats (1st Floor), Navrangpura, Ahmedabad 380009
3-5-1129 Kachiguda Cross Road, Hyderabad 500027
60 Bajaj Nagar, Central Bazar Road, Nagpur 440010
16A Ashok Marg, Patiala House, Lucknow 226001
5th Main Road, Gandhinagar, Bangalore 560009
17 Chittaranjan Avenue, Calcutta 700072
13/14 Asaf Ali Road, New Delhi 110002
751 Anna Salai, Madras 600002

Cover design by Pigments, New Delhi
Cover painting by Thomas Easley in the collection of *The Times of India*

© *Dimensional illustrations* by Thomas Easley

Lasertypeset at Shagun Composers, 92-B, Street 4, Krishna Nagar, Safdarjung Enclave, New Delhi-110 029.

Published by R.N. Sachdev and printed by Ravi Sachdev at Allied Publishers Limited, A-104 Mayapuri II, New Delhi 110064

We must admit at least the possibility,
that everything we believe to be true is
not true.

T.E.

Acknowledgements

This author wishes to thank Chandana Bawa, Samir Jain, Erica Jong, Praveen Kumar and Cris Cassidy. The creation of *The Mechanics of God* would not have been possible without the help and encouragement of these few and dear friends.

And I wish to offer my dedication to Jawala: the Goddess of Fire.

Preface

The first five chapters in this book are brief and basic descriptions of 'The Law of Seven', 'Attention', 'Dimensions', 'The Five Brains', and 'The Law of Three'. They are followed by several diagrams and the 'In Brief' chapter and finally by an alphabetically categorized text.

After reading the first five chapters you may have a question: 'How does the law of seven relate to memory?' Turn to the letter 'M' as you would any dictionary and look up 'Memory'. All subjects addressed here are answered in this way.

God with a capital G refers to that one and only God of religion. God with a small g refers to the powers of creation, as they are understood by metaphysics.

Introduction

Taking the human race to be a mere child: as we must when we consider how young the race is, the question comes to mind—what differences would there be between our immature race and a mature one?

An answer to this question may rest with the laws of Physics and Metaphysics, with time, space, stars, certain rocks, trees, insects like the cockroach and some species of turtle, all of which appear to have reached some degree of maturity. However, since we are not yet able to communicate with such species, we cannot ask them what man may become as a mature race. So our possible maturity must be examined via the state of our immaturity.

Then what are the evidences which illustrate this immaturity? The absence of our sixth sense. Our subjugation to the primitive law of gravity. The unequal status of women. War, the tendency to prejudice and the nationalization of international needs. The fear and misunderstanding of death, fear of the unknown. The need to achieve a sense of security and identity through understanding by definition. Believing there is only one truth, our habitual forgetting. Unproductive or wasted hours of sleep. (Sleep is a labour which produces a tremendous amount of insight, data and energy. Though more than a third of human life is spent in sleep, we generally ignore or disregard sleep as a productive process. It is a little like assuming that nothing happens on the earth when the Sun goes down.)

An immature species is more wasteful, believes in and personalizes God, worries, misunderstands itself and other forms of life, has an inability to read emanations or to project thought, and conceals esoteric doctrines. (An evolved race would have no need for such concealment.) Our inability to remain aware of ourselves in the present, our inability to absorb and understand more than one truth at a time, our mortality, the creation of nonproductive waste, the abuse of nature—these are all signs of our immaturity. As a mature race wonder would dominate our lives, nakedness would clothe us and clothes would reveal our nakedness, sex and love would not confuse or distress us. Tools and the necessities of life, born in the mind, would need only the mind to manufacture them. Animals, plants, germs, insects, the air, time and space would all talk to us and we to them. The list could go and on.

But most of this sounds too fantastic and generally inapplicable to present-day man, and so it is. The human race is not going to mature much in the next fifty to a hundred years. Still there are some things that we can do now in our individual lives that will move the species along, things that can help us guide our merely-living-to-survive state of adaptation toward the more mature state of transformation. *The Mechanics of God* will, I hope, contribute to this process. You can call it a book but it is not really. It's not written to be a book, rather it is a device that makes the act of reading an effort which leads to a practice of what is being read. Any approach that you care to take will suffice. You can read from cover to cover, skip around, read only little bits, start from the back, whatever you want—the process of understanding by observation is built-in. Still it is not possible for me to tell you what to expect; to say exactly what you will get from the book. But one thing I can say is that you must remember to be aware of yourself in the present while you are reading it. If you can do that you will find that our usual tendency to understand by definition is in fact a very clumsy and often inaccurate approach to understanding. (One distinct element that characterizes the difference between adults and small children is that children are less subject to the burden of understanding by definition. They observe, have perception and respond without definition, whereas adults observe, define and then respond; this procedure places the adult's response beyond the moment wherein the observation took place, it moves him further away from the present and the possibility of his being aware of himself in the present. Christ's statement, "Lest ye be as children ..." refers to this state of observation without definition that exists in the child. Adults need to regain that state (the lost continent of their Atlantis) to return to the realm of perception which results from the innocence of having undefined observations. But such an effort would be, and is, difficult for us as we feel great insecurity in the absence of definition, especially in the absence of the definitions "I", "like" and "dislike", which come from the lesser state of adaptation to proclaim themselves to be hallmarks of our individuality and importance.

Once we realize that how we define reality is mostly based on understanding by definition, it shocks us because it means that we know reality primarily as a past experience, since definition follows the present. If we want to live in the present reality, the reality of man's fourth dimension, we need to reduce this tendency to understand by definition. Such an effort would help us personally, it would help the race to evolve our species and it would reduce the senseless conflicts that arise in man from the meeting of contradictory realities within him which he has not yet been able to absorb. A great harmony of contradictions exists in and between the physical and metaphysical worlds. The one unifying thread that connect man to their diverse realities is the present. A man who can live in the present can live in many realities simultaneously, he can harmonize contradictions, he can become whole.

*****

The fourth dimension is the present, the third dimension is the past and the future of the present and the second dimension is the surface of the past and the future. So we live, for the most part, with only a two and three dimensional awareness and with the profound possibility of also having a four-dimensional awareness. Man of the future, (the mature man) will be more four-dimensional and, most likely, five-dimensional. My experience thus far has not provided me with any conclusive information on the fifth dimension. So in *The Mechanics of God* I deal only, and primarily psychologically, with the second, third and fourth dimensions, as all three taken together more accurately represent the "real world" of man, and with the possibility in man of his acquiring the courage to submit to the process of transformation which follows in the absence of definition.

So it would be helpful, when you read this book, to refrain from defining it, from searching for endings. It has taken a great deal of thought and almost twenty years for me to put *The Mechanics of God* together. I would say it is a book for thinking more than a book for reading.

*****

Why did I write it? First because I needed to for myself, for my own effort to sustain an awareness of myself in the present. And secondly, to offer you, the reader—the individual seeking a greater understanding of himself and the world in which we live—a viable alternative or supplement to the group approach to spirituality. I have often heard it said that a single individual on the path to enlightenment cannot get far without help. That may be, but the fractional help that groups can give is not the answer either.

In the beginning a group, even a miscreant group, can assist some by giving the enlistee the seeker, a base or focus for his effort to increase self-awareness and self-knowledge; yet in many cases prolonged membership in a group tends to create a negative elitist attitude in group members toward all people outside the group. Outsiders, because they are without the uniquely divine presence of the group leader, are judged as being less capable or less worthy of enlightenment than are those in the group. Such attitudes cast a veil over the enlistee's much needed critical faculty, divorce him from the reality of his day to day commonness, and significantly dilutes any progress that he may make toward spirituality. What begins for him, upon joining the group, as a ray of hope can imperceptively transform itself into the dark prejudices of a closed society. A society wherein sexual, emotional and financial exploitation by group leaders is common.

Because most of what we can become spiritually is made of what is already inside ourselves and not outside in a group, groups, when they do help, do so by providing some initial organization and energy for our personal work and some knowledge.

So what can we do to protect ourselves from the negative efects of group elitism yet still remain open enough to receive the benefits that a group may have to offer? There are many groups in the market these days, everything from the traditional Zen and Yoga groups to the more unorthodox Gurdjieff groups, EST groups,Channeling groups, Encounter groups, Radiance groups, etc. So the problem is certainly not in finding a group. In fact, many groups even have listings in the phone book. To protect ourselves requires that we stay alert, avoid gross indignities, maintain a resilient yet non-judgemental critical faculty and remember, remember why we have joined a group.

Many people join groups because they are looking for a father or a family that they never had. Others join to get a sense of belonging a sense of camaraderie. Some are just looking for a change, a new experience, entertainment, sex or a spouse. Some people join because they are feeling lost and helpless and some join because they sincerely wish to realize in themselves the full potential of a human being; they wish to "awaken". For those who join for reasons other than "awakening" membership in a group can go on more or less indefinitely, but for those who wish to "awaken" six months to two years is the minimum period and seven to ten years the maximum period of time that they should remain a member. Groups can start the engine of self-examination and self-knowledge, they can teach us the value of directed attention, meditation and love but they can't be those things for us, they can't drive the car. To "awaken" an enlistee must finally embrace life as it is, unconditionally.

Knowing when to leave a group makes the difference between being used by a group or using it. One certain step toward being used is in idolization of the group's leader. Any charismatic person attracts some admiration, because charisma, along with the absence of self-doubt, is most unusual. Yet admiration when it is transformed into idolization gives him who we idolize a dictatorial power over our life. Great huge warning lights should go off in our heads the moment idolization begins. We must regard our time in a group, as we would the occasion of an evening meal. We should know what we want to eat, avoid over-eating or eating too little and be sure not to fall asleep at the table, to get up and walk away when the meal is done. If we cannot walk away from a group with what we have gained while in the group, we must ask ourselves: What have we gained? Knowing when to stand alone is an important step toward spiritual maturity.

My first involvement with groups began when I joined a California based Gurdjieff group. (The Fellowship of Friends) in 1972. I was a typically naive and idealistic youth whose passion for the unknown, for the mysteries of life and death, soon got me into a repressive morass from which I could not extract myself. During my introductory meetings with Fellowship members I was told that I would be in no way bound to the group, that I could leave any time I wanted to. There were no obligations on my part or on the part of the group. That sounded just fine to me so I joined. But it wasn't long, perhaps six to eight months after I made my first payment, before the rules changed. Suddenly I found myself being asked to do things I absolutely did not wish to do, yet I did do them because I had been told that if I did not do them I would be acting against the divine will of the group leader and thereby fail in my search for the mysteries, and if I left the group, even though I had been told I could do so, my spiritual life would go to hell or some place worse. Of course this scenario of intimidation may not be the same for every group; yet some version of it will be there.

Fear tactics such as the ones used on me are typical of the spiritual dictator. Esotericism these days is plagued with a locust of these little Hitlers. One must stay alert; indeed joining a group is almost like slamming into a spider's web and there is little we can do to remain unscathed because the misuse of esoteric doctrines and the various forms of sexual, monetary and psychological exploitation which are common in groups are not illegal. For most group leaders there is nothing inside or outside themselves that can or will prevent them from feeding on their

followers. And once a leader tastes the succulent fruits that power affords
he soon becomes addicted to his pleasures and fails thereafter to see the
pain which he inflicts on his victims.

*****

Throughout *The Mechanics of God* I frequently return to the question
of attention (Is it on yourself in the present, or not?) to the study of
dimensions, to the question of what we can become, what we can see
that we do not see now, what we can learn, what more we can perceive
that we now fail to perceive, how we can expand our view of man's reality.
(The second, the third, and the fourth dimensions are all part of man's
reality—the second houses our shallow attitudes, our vanities, the
indifference in us toward the importance of questioning, doubting and
learning, our addiction to T.V., film and mirrors. The third embraces our
physical life with all its solid truths, pain, joy and labour. The third
dimension is our tangible touchable reality, the flesh-and-blood world
which scientists claim is the only reality for man. The fourth dimension
brings us premonition, strange and magical coincidences, the thought
another person is thinking, the slightly inexplicable state of feeling like
you've been here before, miracles, intuition, out-of-body experiences,
astral projection, etc., etc.)

Over and over and over again we must ask ourselves, "How can I take
the everyday events of my life and transform them into greater self-
awareness?" The present seems so close that we often feel no need to
pursue it. "Of course we are in the present, "we say," where else would
we be?" But when we look closer we notice that we are not in the present,
our attention is not in the present, instead we are lost in our memories
and imaginings about the past and the future. Most of our lives are being
lived presentless. And a man without the present is not a man really as
he is missing the four-dimensional self that makes him whole. To realize
the Self necessities that the individual achieves and maintains a high level
of self-respect and the right functioning of a non-judgemental critical
faculty. He must take responsibility for his need to be aware of himself
in the present, he must become himself the master and the disciple, for
him there can be no waiting or hoping that some divine being other than
himself will come along to drag him out of the ditch. An individual such
as this, one whom I call Self-Religious, cannot permit himself to pawn
off the work he must do himself onto a teacher, God, or other people.
And it may be that such a man can be called a New Age Man, a more
spiritually mature man.

Physics is a science which studies the forces or laws (the electromagnetic force, the strong and weak forces and gravity) which govern nature; the matter and energy of our visible three-dimensional world. The study of forces and laws that govern the invisible four-dimensional world (though the essence of such forces and laws have not yet been agreed upon) is called Metaphysics. And contrary to the opinion of sceptics and the scientific world in general, metaphysics does exist just as the reflection on the opposite side of a window through which we look exists, even if we can't see it (the opposite reflection) when we look through the window.

One man who has contributed much to our general knowledge and awareness of metaphysics was a man named George Gurdjieff. Sometime around 1914 or 1915, in Moscow and St. Petersburg, Russia, Gurdjieff introduced a remarkable body of esoteric knowledge entitled THE SYSTEM. Over the past seventy years Gurdjieff's system has been expanded upon, sometimes for the better, sometimes for the worse, by many of his followers. Books by P.D. Ouspensky, Rodney Collin, John Bennet, Maurice Nicoll, Alexander Horn and Joel Friedlander represent some of the better books written about system ideas. *The Mechanics of God: A Theory on the Transition of Species and Events*, like its predecessors builds on essential truths of the Gurdjieff System, hopefully for the better.

Contents

Chapter one

The Law of Seven

The law of seven (the Interval Law) is common to both material and immaterial realities. Thus its field of influence impersonally influences many dimensions just as gravity of the third dimension impersonally influences many diverse species and events within the third dimension.

The law of seven as I received it, employed the European major scale to give it definition. I had planned to use the major scale in my presentation of the law of seven but discovered that people's previous understanding of music interfered with the explanation. For purposes of clarification I have chosen then to substitute the term 'note' with the term 'quanta'. Thus we have in the original, the notes do-re-mi (interval) fa-sol-la-si (interval) do-re- etc.etc. replaced by quanta one (Q1), quanta two (Q2), quanta three (Q3), (interval) quanta four (Q4), quanta five (Q5), quanta six (Q6), quanta seven (Q7), interval, quanta one, two, three, etc. etc. A total of seven notes and two intervals make up one octave—this is changed to seven quantas and two intervals making up one series.

A completed series results when all seven quantas unite after successfully passing both intervals.

A quanta (as defined here) represents a unit of energy which has a definite yet abstract momentum following an irresistible course dictated by the boundaries of the law of seven.

Once quanta one has been energized, quanta two and three, by absolute association, must follow.

Upon entering the first interval, the Q3-Q4 interval, the related identities of quanta one, quanta two and quanta three lose contact temporarily or entirely with that course originally dictated to them.

The related and individual identities of these quantas can remain in the interval indefinitely, can pass through the interval intact, go backwards, enter another series in another interval and change direction, or disperse utterly into some unknown.

If the first interval is passed and quanta four energizes, quanta five, six and seven must follow. The successful passage of a related series of seven quantas through the second (Q7-Q1) interval, wherein similar, yet greater difficulties than in the first interval arise, means that the identity of the entire series has become complete, has entered into and passed out of the diabolic uncertainties of the interval.

A series, thus intact, is now at liberty to further its identity, to develop into a recurring series singly or collectively by association with other like species and events and/or, to produce as offspring, the Q1 quanta of another series.

Because of the abstract nature of the quanta, it is difficult to observe a series quanta by quanta, so observation and verification of the law of seven begins with observing the intervals.

A common example of the first interval of a day series is the afternoon nap. You start your day feeling as if you will get through it successfully. And so you do, through the first three quantas. Then something starts to happen. You go to work, but the reason for being on the job begins to lose importance, there must be better things to do. Day-dreaming sets in and you fill your mind with images of other places. And there is tiredness; that seeping in of strong urges to sleep-sleep-sleep. You look at the clock—it is eleven-thirty, noon, quarter-past-twelve, or maybe two- or three-thirty. The exact time doesn't really matter. What does matter is the fact that you can't stop yourself from feeling the lull when the first interval of your day arrives.

The interval is an absolute and irresistible force in the life of all three-dimensional species and events. It must happen, it does happen and it will happen. Were this not so, we would work non-stop, the sun would never set, rain would never fall or once begun never stop. We couldn't die if we were alive, or be born if we were dead. Without the interval, change of any kind would not exist. Even when we decide that we want change, change is not possible until an interval arrives. Try all you will to stop crying, before the interval comes you won't be able to. 'Oh, stop the pain,' you say, 'I don't want to feel this.' You can't stop it no matter how great your wish to do so. The pain will stay until the interval is reached. But the interval means only that something can change, not that something will change.

There is an element of choice in the interval; an awareness of possibilities, which helps us recognize the arrival of the interval. People who are able to accomplish their goals all have either a built-in or learned ability to recognize the arrival of the interval and a comprehension of what to do to pass it.

The interval is profound, awesome. Creation of all that we know to be life could not have happened without it. The plants, the solar system, bugs, the time of day, rushing rivers, deep seas, the mystery of migration, childbirth. For all of these to begin an interval in pre-existing species and events was needed.

Realization of choice and the sense to choose wisely are two blessings bestowed upon human nature. A rock, a tree, a fish, in being less aware of choice, have fewer choices—thus fewer possibilities of initiating change. And a man who could be aware of choice, yet is not, is less than a rock, in that he has possibilities which he fails to recognize. A rock, in having little choice, cannot fail because failure is not a possibility.

The second interval, (Q7-Q1), which is often more difficult than the first, follows the successful sounding of the last four quantas. It is more difficult for several reasons. Generally, there is a greater sense of urgency surrounding the second interval, because the successful completion of the entire series is at stake. And the need to make the right choice puts pressure on whoever is responsible. Expectations are high, risk is greater, a choice must be made. The second interval represents the difference between success and failure, the difference between understanding and ignorance. An ignorant man is so because he rarely takes an idea, a dream, a question all the way to its conclusion. He is satisfied with mediocrity, partial understanding, partial success, partial truth. No understanding can be complete, no dream realized, no question answered, no child born before passing the second interval. The second interval represents the hard part, the difficulties of finishing something.

Continuing with my earlier example of the first interval being the nap, the second interval or slump time comes somewhere nearer to the evening, before leaving the office, before dinner, before stopping at the bar, when one feels too tired to go on and thought loses its sharpness. A sense of worn hopelessness can set in or its opposite, a compelling urge to push on, to finish at all costs, that last step of whatever one is doing.

Many people have automobile accidents close to their homes because they become careless and hurry through the second interval near the end of the series. If we chose to we could blame many a missed date, tardy party goer, careless mishap and goof-up on slump time.

Another example of the two intervals, taken on a larger scale, are the present changes occurring in the Russian communist system. Some time before Nikita Khrushchev came to power a mood, a need to re-examine and readjust that system began to form the first interval. Khrushchev's removal from power was the shock used to pass the first interval before a change of direction could be made. This meant that the original series, the Communist series, would continue intact and that no other attempt to change the original series could take place until the second interval. Mikhail Gorbachev has arrived at the time of the second interval. If he fails to change the series in the second interval it will become impossible to sound the first quanta of a new series. In the absence of the first quanta in a new series the old series will develop into an indefinite recurring series. It could take many many years before such an opportunity arises again, so it is very important for an improvement in the lives of the Russian people that Gorbachev succeed.

The law of seven can be observed and verified on many scales. From the behaviour of the smallest atom and cell to that of the largest black hole or universe. Yet certainly the most important observations and verifications for us to make are those seen in the world of our day-today existence. An awareness of this law in our daily lives can contribute to a greater level of success and a deeper understanding of all that we do. It may be that you are about to lose hope or patience but you realize that you are in the second interval and that if you just hang on a bit longer things will work out. Or you see that it is necessary to pause for a while because you are in the first interval and you can't continue on to quanta four until the first interval is passed. Or perhaps you are procrastinating, hesitating over something you know you need to do. This means that your attention is still caught up in something unresolved in the second interval of another series. If you know this it is easier to say 'OK let's get on with what we have to do.' Also critical and judgmental attitudes towards oneself and other people are reduced because there is no one to blame for the interruptions, the pauses, the brakes in routine caused by the arrival of an interval.

For example—you and your wife are having an intimate dinner together when a call comes from your mother-in-law in New York. An interval had to occur, that it was your mother-in-law is only incidental. Or your child enters the room crying while you are still in bed. The child is not to blame. A string breaks on your guitar, you get a flat tyre, it rains, the dog wets on the floor, you stub your toe, the guard falls asleep. The law of seven, like a great ocean which stands behind the making of a drop of sea water is the cause.

At first it is difficult to realize that the law of seven is constant in our lives, just as gravity is constant. One important difference between the law of gravity and the law of seven is that the law of seven has an influence on the fourth dimension whereas gravity has little or no influence. This means that the law of seven affects us when we are living and when we are dead, influences both the body and the soul. And it is of great importance to realize that the intervals in the law of seven provide us with a doorway that leads to the fourth-dimension. It is, in fact, just these intervals in the law of seven that make it possible for four dimensional beings and laws to enter our world of the third dimension. All truly new ideas, new species and events are a result of forces from the fourth dimension entering the third. Quite simply, we would not exist without the interval, as the possibility of creating us would not exist.

There are many keys to unlock the door to the fourth dimension, but there is only one door, and that door is the interval.

It is more difficult for three-dimensional beings and powers to enter the fourth dimension than it is for four-dimensional beings and powers to enter the third. For a man to transform his being, by will, through the interval into the fourth dimension he must live for a period of time in the interval. *This means that he must live without definition.* One constant characteristic of the interval is the absence of definition. In a state of pure possibility there can be no identity. For a man who gains a sense of himself by way of recognized habits and tendencies, (quantas), for a man who sees himself defined as a man (a connected multiple recurring series), as we all do, it is very difficult to cast off, even briefly, this socially accepted view. Yet it is this accepted view that keeps man from even momentary exposure to life on the other side. Also too much accidental time in an interval can produce what we call insanity. Someone who experiences life without a human identity—if he has not been prepared for this—can no longer relate normally to those who see life only in relation to human identity. Life in the interval can be a confused and disturbing experience, but without it there can be no transition of species and events.

One additional point to note about the interval is that a shock of some kind is needed to pass the interval. Many arguments between married couples are good examples of this. Let us take the case of Sally and John Smith. Sally has called John at work to ask him what he would like for dinner, the first quanta (Q1) of the phone call series. John is occupied with a problem so he gives Sally a quick and thoughtless answer— 'noodle soup' (Q2). Sally knows that John has no real interest in noodle soup so she points that out to John, (Q3). John loses patience and tells Sally he does not care what she makes for dinner. Sally then says this is typical of John's lack of interest in her— he does not care what she makes for dinner, how she dresses, where she wants to go for a vacation, how she feels about anything. John says that she is over-reacting. Back and forth they go; the (Q3-Q4) interval is in progress. The shock which helps to pass the (Q3-Q4) interval comes in the form of John's secretary telling him that his biggest client is on the other line. John tells Sally that he will call her right back. Five minutes later he calls her back (Q4). Sally asks him once again what he would like for dinner (Q5). John says noodle soup and hamburgers (Q6). Sally asks how would he like his hamburger, well done, medium, or rare (Q7). John says he does not care how the hamburger is done. Sally says he does not care about the noodles, the hamburger or her, and that she does not care if he comes home for dinner, or if he comes home at all. John tells her to stop making a big deal out of nothing. Sally says that John has been saying that for the entire ten years they have been married. Back and forth they go —the (Q7-Q1) interval is in progress and it will continue until a shock comes to bridge the interval.

That intervals arrive and deviations occur can be observed continuously throughout the day. In fact as I'm sitting here writing this an interval is occurring. This interval is not visible to you because I'm filling it with these words. It began hours ago, just minutes after the Sally and John conversation. I wanted to give you another example of the interval. As I began to write what I'm writing now another idea came to me. It seemed important so I stopped and wrote it down. This pause gave way to a longer deviation when Meera's son asked to play a computer game with me. Once the game was over I returned to continue with my example but felt so tired I couldn't write. My eyes kept trying to close (I'd slept only three hours the night before) and my mind kept wandering without a focus. Five minutes later a car pulled up to take me to the office. Eight hours later I'm back home in front of my typewriter closing the gap. I've passed the (Q3-Q4) interval in the series of writing this example. Upon completing this chapter I also complete this series, pass the (Q7-Q1) interval and move on to the next chapter, the next series.

And this is how it goes. We are always losing sight of our attention, leaving conversations unfinished, forgetting what we were doing or saying, writing half letters, believing half truths, dreaming half dreams.

Chapter two

Attention

Attention in man is that energy produced by him which gives identity to his consciousness.

The usual state of man's attention is scattered and undirected. We live in this way more by accident than by choice. To focus attention, to give choice to the identity of our consciousness, requires that we first find our attention. The best place and time to look for attention is now, in this moment, wherever you are, doing whatever you are doing. So where is it? Lost in thoughts about the future, what to do, where to go, who to see or is it in memories of the past, lovelorn longings, resentments, pleasures? Are you thinking about someone in the other room who is talking too loud? Are you focused on what you are reading and asking yourself questions about this subject? Are you imagining foods you want to eat? Is your mind wandering off to the kitchen? Is the chair you're sitting in uncomfortable? The day too hot, or cold? Is your attention bouncing about controlled moment to moment by the subject most strongly attracting it? What we need to do is find our attention, then direct it toward what we understand to be in any given moment our greatest profit, to keep it from being taken by things, events, other people.

Though attention is produced by us it is rarely controlled by us. So the identity of our consciousness is often not our own, rather it is the identity of that which we have given our attention to. A hamburger, a beautiful painting, a religion, a watch, a pretty girl, a new car, a prayer, an argument, a song, etc., all attract attention and identity.

Man's understanding of what is good for him differs from person to person. Thus the focus of attention differs from person to person. To focus

on a game, lunch, or a good book, in the beginning matters very little.
What matters most is to discover where attention is and attempt to focus
it on the present. Only with the focus of our attention on the present can
we gain the concentrated energy necessary to press the identity of our
consciousness through the intervals in the law of seven into the fourth
dimension: the heaven of man. I know this sounds too simple. Just focus
your attention on the present and you go to Heaven. It is that simple and
not that simple. It requires great strength to focus attention on the present
and there are many obstacles internal and external which challenge us:
forces in the world which prey on our attention as a cat preys on a mouse.

Once we have become accustomed to asking ourselves, 'Where is my
attention now?' we can begin to ask, 'What shall I do with this attention?'
If we give it to sport we could become decent athletes, if we give it
to business we could become good businessmen. Giving it to family
makes a better family, to mathematics a better mathematician. All
professionalism is based on the giving of attention to a specific interest
or talent.

So we can say that there is attention, and there is that on which the
attention is focused. The unification of the two produces awareness of
our being where we are, doing what we are doing. At first the presence
of this awareness is quite strange, but we get accustomed to it the more
we attempt to maintain it.

Then there is the unpredictable arrival of the Observer: the non-
participating perception of invisible being.
     The process which precedes the arrival of the Observer begins with
our effort to locate and direct attention and to carry that attention past
both intervals in the law of seven in the third dimension. Once we have
begun this effort to become aware of where we are, the first three quantas
of the law of seven follow obediently, like sheep after sheep. We feel
in this succession a slight ray of hope. But then the first (Q3-Q4) interval
arrives and we are distracted. This is usually where we stop. If we are
a bit stronger we can carry on through this interval and past the next
four quantas. At the second interval, the (Q7-Q1) interval, we meet a
greater challenge and a greater reward. Distractions in the second interval
seem more real, more urgent, more important than the effort to remain

aware of ourselves in the present. Yet if we persevere with bridging the second interval our awareness can pass into the Observer and enter through an intersecting interval in the law of seven into the Observer's world of the fourth dimension. From the Observer's vantage point we can peer through the interval in the fourth dimension and its consecutive intersecting interval in the third dimension, into the third dimension. Then we see this world as it would be seen by the saints.

How long the Observer will stay cannot be known (usually it stays for brief periods of time only, long periods would be difficult for us to bear) as its presence signifies the transformation of human being into inhuman and nonhuman being.

Diverse dimensions and beings of dimensions, mating, procreating pure life, miracles, time itself, new worlds, the mysteries: it all seems so wonderful yet so distant. Talk of heaven, enlightenment, life after death, god. These are just words for realities kept from us most of our lives because we cannot bear to look in a mirror and see that there is no one there—no individual person who is personally favoured by the earth and the universe and god. In fact, it is just this illusion that we are favoured that is our greatest barrier and obstacle to maintaining an awareness of our attention in the present. And without this awareness, the ordinary miracles of our day-to-day lives remain spectacles of wonder for the gods only.

Chapter three

Dimensions

I remember being fascinated as a child with the fact that things disappeared. Clouds in the sky disappeared, the sun disappeared, people that walked around corners disappeared, winter— after the melting snow—vanished. Where did they go? How could something so large as a season or the night sky fade that completely? As I grew up I learned that reality had many faces depending upon which dimension I was most aware of.

Man, as a material creation, is understood to be a three-dimensional being. Thus the second dimension lies just below him and the fourth just above. Put quite simply, the second dimension is a flat world represented, in part, by photographs, paintings, TV and movie screens, mirrored reflection, surfaces, etc. The third dimension is a world of solids, and space between solids, a world of weighty material species and events— the fundamental reality of which man is most aware. The fourth dimension is the time body of the third dimension. And four-dimensional beings are those beings made of the time taken in the third dimension to fulfil the entire process of a lifetime of a three-dimensional species or event. For example a man is conceived, he is born, lives, and dies. The whole of his lifetime is his time body, the body of a four-dimensional being or a fragment of a time body in the fourth dimension.

All species and events within the fourth dimension are under different laws from those in the third, or those in the second. What we call the past and the future do not exist in the fourth dimension. Time as a linear process does not exist. Gravity, electro-magnetism, the strong force and the weak force either do not exist or they have almost no effect.

It is difficult for us to imagine a world without time, gravity or death. But we don't need to imagine it. With effort and a little luck we can experience it.

An aspect of being in the fourth dimension is seeing the third and second dimensions from the fourth dimension. For example, if I see a tree from within the fourth dimension I see the lifetime of that tree, the lifetime of a cat, the lifetime of a man. The seeing of lifetimes can be described as an awareness or a perception of energies. The lifetime of a tree will not be a still or slightly moving material. It will be a dynamic fluctuation of all those forces which have acted upon it throughout its entire three-dimensional existence. This, awareness of energies, can also be understood as digestion of emanations.

We, as three-dimensional beings, are frequently and unknowingly stimulated by the receiving of emanations, or energies flowing from the fourth dimension. At some time in the distant future scientists will arrive at the need and the ability to measure the effect of emanations on the life of man. At this time emanations are not even taken into consideration. Science cannot yet see beyond the speed of light. An individual devoted to focusing his attention on himself, in the present, can.

The fourth dimension is much more powerful than the third dimension, just as the third dimension is more powerful than the second. In the second dimension, the world of the plane, it's quite clear to us that we, as three-dimensional beings can completely control and destroy any being, photograph, painting, reflection, etc., in the second dimension. We cannot destroy the dimension itself but we are the certain masters over creations within it. The fourth dimension has this same relationship to us. Any four-dimensional being, or even the laws of the fourth dimension, can control and destroy any three-dimensional being.

Most concepts of God are based on our misunderstanding and fear of the laws and beings of the fourth dimension. To assume that the influence of the fourth dimension can be reduced to one all-embracing Grand Unification Theory, as some scientists do, or one all-powerful God, as many religious leaders do, is naive and immature. There is a great difference between the three-dimensional concept of divinity as a loving warlord flying along in puffy clouds, surrounded by angels and spirits, and the four-dimensional reality of utterly non-human and inhuman beings who know us as mere spurts of energy with some possible usefulness.

Religions that claim numerous and diverse gods are closer to the truth, yet far from our need to replace illusions with verifiable facts.

Chapter four

The Five Brains

A multi-functional five-brain being is not exactly the picture we have of Man. An upright, two-legged, single-headed builder of bridges and maker of heroes is much closer. How can we call ourselves 'modern' with so antique an understanding of man? Certainly we should know more about ourselves than we do about any other species or events, but we do not.

The mistaken idea, laid down in the Old Testament, that man was created in the image of one God has devastated the real image of man by permitting us to believe that man is one. Man was created in parts with the parts of many species to serve as a multi-functional channel for the finer energies of the third dimension to pass into and nourish aspects of the growth of beings in the fourth dimension. For man to succeed at this purpose he was endowed not with one brain, but with five brains: five centres of intelligence.

The five brains of man, each with its own distinct influence on the life of man are these—the Intellectual brain, the Moving brain, the Instinctive brain, the Emotional brain, and the Unifier brain. All people are centred (born with a propensity to establish values and interests predominantly in one of these brains) in either the Intellectual, Moving, Instinctive or Emotional brains. No one is centred in the Unifier. Diagrams illustrating the parts of these brains can be found in the common deck of playing cards (see diagrams 3, 4, 5, 6 & 7).

The Intellectual brain, which has its physical centre located in the head, represents that side of man where logic resides. This brain has the slowest rate of comprehension, is the brain least capable of responding spontaneously to new situations. It is the storehouse of literal facts and numbers: most experiences processed by this brain must be reduced to a logical non-abstract reason. We are deeply limited in our understanding of man and the world in which he lives when we attempt to reason only via those processes associated to the Intellectual brain. All beliefs and convictions established by this brain are either absolute or either-or. All mental habits, such as slogans, cliches, standard jokes and catch words come from it. Yet it is possible, through the use of the higher parts of the Intellectual brain (the 8, 9 and 10 of diamonds), to comprehend that knowledge, buried in the ages, which reveals to man how important and how possible it is to arrive at the door of the fourth dimension. All great words of wisdom have come to man via the higher parts of the Intellectual brain. All truly new ideas must pass through this same door. And we experience our most profound understanding when the higher parts of both the Intellectual and Emotional brains and the Unifier work together.

Next we have the Moving brain. All learned movement is developed here. Our ability to walk, to form words of speech, to move from place to place, to practise and enjoy sport and dance are Moving brain activities. The profession of ballet dancing is populated primarily by those whose lives are dominated by the functioning of the Moving brain.

The rate of digestion of experiences, impressions, food, etc. is the means by which we measure the speed, or time of each brain: how quickly a brain comprehends something. The Moving brain, for example, has a rate of digestion 30,000 times faster than that of the Intellectual brain. What this means is that the Moving brain can have and understand many experiences, where the Intellectual brain may have only one. If I took a ball and threw it to you unexpectedly you would use your Moving brain to catch it. You would not need to think, 'Now here comes a ball that weighs two ounces and is travelling at a speed of eight miles per hour; to catch it I will need to extend my right hand out at the rapid pace of twenty miles per hour and I must open my hand to its full capacity to create a large enough catching surface.' Instead, you just catch the ball. If the Intellectual brain were asked to catch the ball it would need a week to figure out how to do that.

Awareness of spatial relations is also a part of the Moving brain's world. When we walk through a room or down the street, or look up at the night sky, our ability to avoid running into objects and people, to distinguish

the differences and distances between things, is made possible by the
Moving brain. All the images in our dreams come from the Moving brain.
Pleasure of movement, and the raw need to exercise, are the Moving brain.

The Instinctive brain and the Moving brain have the same rate of digestion,
but the Instinctive brain has more power over the influence of digestion.
This means that energy manufactured in the physical body by the
absorption of experiences and food is directed by the Instinctive brain
to sustain, at all costs, the life force of the physical body. The Moving
brain must act in harmony with the dictates of the Instinctive brain, not
independent from it. The Instinctive brain can and does act independently
of the Moving brain.

Digestion of experiences in the Moving brain produce that energy in the
physical body, directed by the Moving brain which gives the physical
body motion. Such experiences and digestion in being so frequently
subordinated to the needs of the Instinctive (physical) brain, give the
impression that the Moving brain is less serious, less important than the
Instinctive brain, even though they have the same rate of digestion. People
who are centred in the Moving brain are often seen by others as being
non-serious; whereas people who are centred in the Instinctive brain are
viewed as serious, even threatening. Only those people who are *centred*
in the Moving brain can override the Instinctive brain's control over
digestion.
    Moving-centred people can ignore hunger, tiredness or pain if they
are sufficiently involved in moving-centred activity like skiing, dancing,
running, etc., while an Instinctive type would not be able to ignore hunger,
tiredness or pain in the same situations.

Other aspects of the Instinctive brain and centre are the five senses and
the material substance and form of the physical body. It is a big job for
the Instinctive brain to run the physical body. People who are centred
in the Instinctive brain are most aware of instinctive needs, and most
capable of fulfilling those needs. The other brains can forget to sleep,
eat, or have sex. But the Instinctive brain rarely forgets.

The lower part of the Instinctive brain coordinates the process of digesting what we eat and drink and it is responsible for the reliability of the heartbeat, lymph system and the immune system.

Secrecy, caution, fear and what we often call psychic perception or ESP (Extra Sensory Perception) are aspects of the intelligence of the higher part of the Instinctive brain (the King of Clubs). Most human fears, that is, fears of imagined dangers or difficulties, are not legitimate fears. For fear to be legitimate in the human body, it must come from the Instinctive brain.

The king of clubs also represents the instinctive intelligence in mankind which regulates the behaviour of the masses of people. A city or country would not survive if all their people converged on the same street corner, shop, movie house, beach, river, or hill all at the same time. No man, company, armed force or federal law can give order to a city. For the regulation of behaviour the king of clubs must be involved. Huge riots and revolutions arise when the Emotional brain overpowers the regulating effects of the Instinctive brain. The king of clubs is a brilliant organizer and strategist whose powers and strengths are often mistaken for spiritual powers and strengths.

Here are some examples of the Emotional brain over-powering the Instinctive brain.

One day in Italy a famous Italian actress was giving acting lessons to a group of young students. One of the girls was overwhelmed emotionally by being in the presence of her idol. The girl fainted and her heart stopped beating. She was revived by the teacher and sent home. From this we can see that the Instinctive centre is not wrong in fearing strong emotional experiences as such experiences could kill it.

Hitler moved the world to great sorrow by his emotional manipulation of the masses. How many people die each year for an idea, a faith, a love of freedom. The hundreds of young people who starved themselves in Beijing is another good example where the Instinctive centre's desire to defend and protect itself has been subordinated to an emotionally charged dream.

One difficulty that doctors and scientists encounter in studying the human brain is that they do not realize that five brains share the material of that single brain. The Intellectual, Moving, Instinctive, Emotional and Unifying brains all have interchangeable energies, functions and parts. It takes a good deal of observation to see how they work separately. As long as those who research the function of the brain do so without consideration of the other processes of intelligence in the body, they will come up with only vague and partial explanations of the behaviour of man.

The Emotional brain is the least developed brain of the five—mainly because we give most of our life force to the Instinctive brain's need to orchestrate our survival here on this very dusty and rugged planet. Were we free of great instinctive demands, the Emotional brain would have more energy to express and develop its perceptions of human reality. The Instinctive brain fears strong emotional experiences because they pose a threat to its health and safety. This fear of emotion, which usually begins when we are quite young, retards the development of the Emotional brain, which, in turn, reduces the depth and quality of our perceptions. The higher part of the Emotional brain (the King of Hearts) receives and digests impressions and emanations with an ability to discriminate between them moment by moment. When the Emotional brain has been retarded by unjust fears, this ability is kept from us.

Faith and belief are emotional strangulation. The Instinctive brain supports belief because belief guarantees a comfortable pasture for the Instinctive centre to graze in— the promise of a purposeful life on Earth and a life after death. Challenging perceptions coming from the Emotional brain are labelled blasphemous and questioning is subdued. With the illusions of faith and belief all fears are covered over by a warm and suffocating sleep.

Sensations and feelings are difficult to separate. Often when we say that we feel good or that we feel bad, happy or in love, we think we're being emotional. We fail to realize that these feelings are more sensation than feeling because we are not aware of them at the point where they enter the emotional brain as perception. We become aware of them only when they arrive in the Instinctive centre and we sense a physically useful or a non-useful relationship to them. If a relationship is one of usefulness we say I feel good, I'm in love, I'm happy; if not, we say that I feel bad. But these are not feelings because they are not based on the conditions which increase emotional perception; instead they are based on their utility to the survival of the Instinctive brain. For a feeling to be an emotion there must be within the feeling itself a perception of where that feeling has come from and where it could go. There must be a discriminatory understanding that will tell you if that feeling can lead to more and greater possibilities of enlightenment or reduced possibilities. Sensations do not include this very important aspect. Discrimination in the instinctive world, as I stated before, is related to survival of the body, not to the nourishment of the soul.

A further understanding of the differences between feelings and sensations can be observed by comparing the weightlessness of perception to the weight of attachment in sensations. Sensations hold us down, perceptions help us to rise. For instance I have the perception: an emotional realization, that someone is lying to me yet I believe him because the sensation of his confidence and smile has fooled me. Trust, however, is not a characteristic of perception. We might perceive that someone cannot be trusted but the feeling of trust is a sensation that frequently gets us into trouble because the Instinctive centre does not mind subjecting us to a little pain if the pain helps to distract the Emotional brain from having new perceptions. If we could follow our hearts more often than we follow our sensations heaven would be much closer and exploitation a lesser possibility.

The fifth brain—the Unifier—is the least physical, the least tangible of the five brains as it has no physical divisions. Its principal function is to supply the fine energy of harmony to all the brains as equally as possible. Unfortunately, this most wonderful function is rarely set in motion, as the fine energy of the Unifier is usually siphoned off little by little by the greed and habits of the lower parts of the other four brains. (Most people spend the greater part of their lives in the jacks of centres. The jacks account for almost all habits, and the queens account for most of our greed.) Were we able to make better use of the higher parts of the four brains (the kings), the fifth brain would have more of an opportunity to perform its good deeds.

The Unifier's work of harmonizing the diverse processes of the Intellectual, Moving, Instinctive, and Emotional brains can result in an integration of that harmony with the greater world of the fourth dimension; the realization of man's greatest dreams, his transformation of the flesh into spirit.

Our most vibrant, sensitive, and explosive moments can be attributed to the production of fine energy of the Unifier. The Unifier is the seat of our common sense as it produces the only energy equally common to all the brains. *When we lack common sense we lack the prowess of the decision-making process of the Unifier.*

The speed of digestion of the Unifier is the fastest of all the brains, therefore the closest to a higher dimension. The speed of digestion of the Emotional brain is 30,000 times faster than that of the Moving and Instinctive brains and the Unifier is that much faster than the Emotional brain. These speeds are difficult to verify in a logical manner because to do so would require the work of the slowest brain, the Intellectual brain. It would be like asking a bicycle to explain the function and purpose of a spaceship. To verify the speeds of these brains and to witness the processes of their functioning we need to locate our attention and direct it toward an awareness of ourselves, where we are, doing whatever we are doing, (see Brains).

All higher possibilities for man depend very much on his gaining access to those strengths associated with the higher parts of each of the five brains, the kings, because it is the kings who distribute the energy of the Unifier, emanations, and food to all the parts beneath them. Usually it is the lower parts, the habits, which are in control.

The five brains, which make up a large segment of the human being, are perceived differently by the fourth dimension than by the third. Viewed from the fourth dimension, a human being is not one body: instead there are pulses of energy intermixing in a blend that either receives from other species and events, or acts upon them. When these energies are slowed down or subdued by too rigid beliefs or actions, they are seen as non-life. Thus a man who has become inflexible, a man who has defined absolutely what life is, when viewed from the fourth dimension, can look no different from the energy of a stone. Death to the human being does not occur with the destruction of the body, but with the degeneration of nourishment for the soul. This can occur well before the death of the body.

Chapter five

The Law of Three

Active, passive and neutralizing forces make up the visible side of the *Law of three*. Yet they do not give us access to the intelligence behind them which relates them to each other as a manifestation of the law of three. To observe the mind behind the law of three we would need to be completely free of the third dimension. As it is now we must try to understand by studying traces. The law of three is essentially that action or force which ignites change. Active, passive, and neutralizing energies are employed by that force either separately, collectively or in combinations.

The best place to observe the law of three is in the interval of the law of seven. Let's take the example of a man fishing. He has been sitting on the shore without catching a fish for two hours; quantas one, two and three have been sounded. At the end of two hours he received a tiny nibble so now he can't decide whether to stay or leave. This indecision places him in the first interval. Some voices in his head say go, others say wait, wait because that fish could bite. No don't wait, this is just a waste of time. You could do much better on the other side of the lake. So his thoughts go back and forth and back and forth dualistically circling in his head. Active-passive, passive-active, active-passive and they continue in this way until a neutralizing force, the third force, sent in by the law of three, shocks them into either an active or passive action. Without the law of three a shock to the interval would not happen and everything would remain as it is, unchanged. The law of three plays a role in the passing of every interval in the law of seven. So here is our fisherman, he has just been touched by the neutralizing force: the third force combining with the first force (active) and the second force (passive) to establish a manifestation of the law of three. The thought comes to him, 'I'm hungry'. This thought causes his mouth to taste a hamburger, fries, and a milkshake; so he stands up, packs his bag and walks away. The interval has been passed. Intuitively we know that a third force, a third part or party is needed to resolve any yes/no, right/wrong situation.

On a larger scale there are events like the present dialogue between Iran and Iraq. This dialogue could not take place between these two forces without the help of a third force, a neutralizing third party. This third force, a principal actor on the stage of change in the transition of any species or event, has the power to turn a species or event toward the realm of greater possibilities, ascent toward enlightenment, or toward the realm of lesser possibilities, descent away from enlightenment.

If an action within the interval of a series is designated by the law of three to ascend after the interval, the series will ascend. The law of three in this way acts as the hand of God but it is not God, rather it is a four-dimensional law that has frequent and direct participation in the world of the third dimension. The lapping over of this law into the third dimension is often mistaken for God as its effect can make the difference between a species or event ascending or descending, between life and death. When the effect is one of ascent this means that the first quanta in the law of seven, which is sounded after passing the Q7-Q1 interval, will lead the following quantas on an ascending course. If the shock applied by the law of three at the beginning is great enough, both the Q3-Q4, and the Q7-Q1 intervals will be passed quite easily and the species or event will continue to ascend. This same process is true in the reverse when the force of the law of three pushes a series down toward the realm of fewer possibilities. Any descending series of quantas in the law of seven can be reversed in any of the intervals which that series encounters, just as any ascending series can be made to descend in its intervals. There are no guarantees on the road to enlightenment. We always want guarantees and religious leaders always tell us there are guarantees. But no man not even a Jesus Christ or a Buddha, can guarantee the behaviour of the law of three.

One way to reduce the inadvertent power that the law of three has on our lives is by developing *will*: an internal being that replaces the law of three as the third force which acts to fill the intervals in the law of

THE LAW OF THREE

seven. This can be done, but it is the most difficult task that a man can place before himself. An enlightened will, one which has the power to dominate the interval, implies that a three-dimensional man has created within himself, a being of the fourth dimension. With the influence of this four dimensional being in hand, a man can have some guarantee of success over the power of the law of three, but this guarantee is not absolute.

(I would like to pause for a moment now and ask you, once again, to check for the whereabouts of your attention, to grab hold of it and coax it to remain here with you wherever you are while you are reading these words. There is no past in this present moment and there is no future.)

Since the law of three is that deciding force which interconnects the five brains to produce an action, it becomes clear why it is so difficult to say exactly which brain is responsible for an action, that is, why we behave the way we do.

Let's say you're John standing at the front door of Sally's house with a bunch of flowers in your hand. While you're standing there, you're thinking why you should apologize. It was Sally that started the argument. You can't decide whether to ring the bell or not. Your Instinctive brain is saying to do it because it wants to make love to Sally. In this moment the Instinctive brain is the active force. The Emotional brain is the passive force; it is saying don't do it because she should apologize first. The other three brains are all present, but they're in the neutral position. In the next moment the Instinctive brain takes the passive position and the Emotional brain the neutral. But then the Emotional brain doesn't agree so it moves to the active position and tells you to walk away. The Intellectual brain attempts to move into the active position, but is stopped by the Moving brain which rings the bell. So you can see from this how difficult it is to say exactly at which moment which brain is chosen to create an action.

It is difficult to verify that the impersonal manifestation of a mostly invisible law decides our actions. That we are, quite simply, associative stimulus-response beings. Our belief that we decide what is right and wrong, good or bad, that we choose to like or dislike is a misconception. Duality is a reactionary force, not a deciding force. Man is dualistic, he lives—he dies, he gets hot—he gets cold, he loves—he hates, he stops—he starts, he does not choose to act—he has chosen to act. Then the question to ask is 'how can I become the deciding force.'

DIAGRAM ONE
A Multiple Intersecting Interval

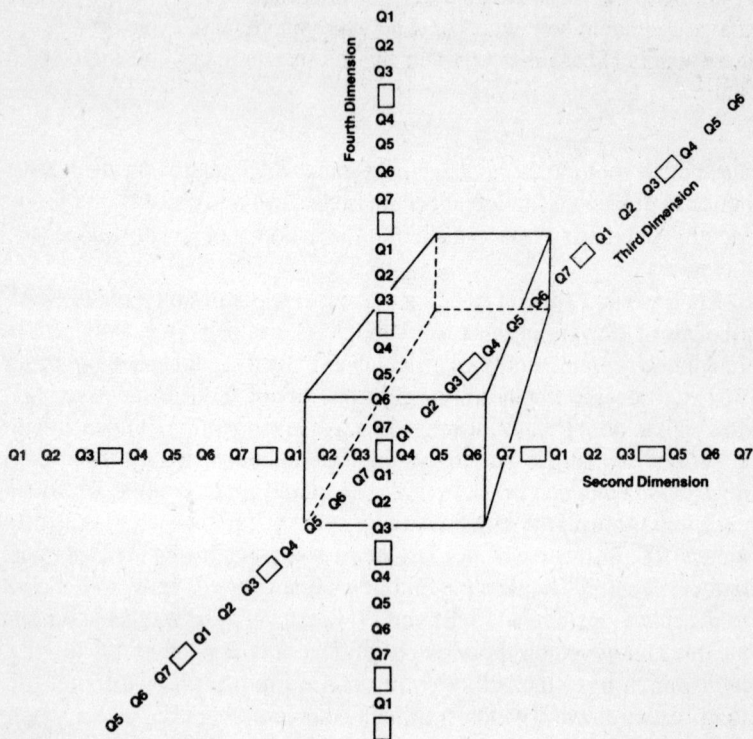

DIAGRAM TWO

A Consecutive Intersecting Transitional Interval

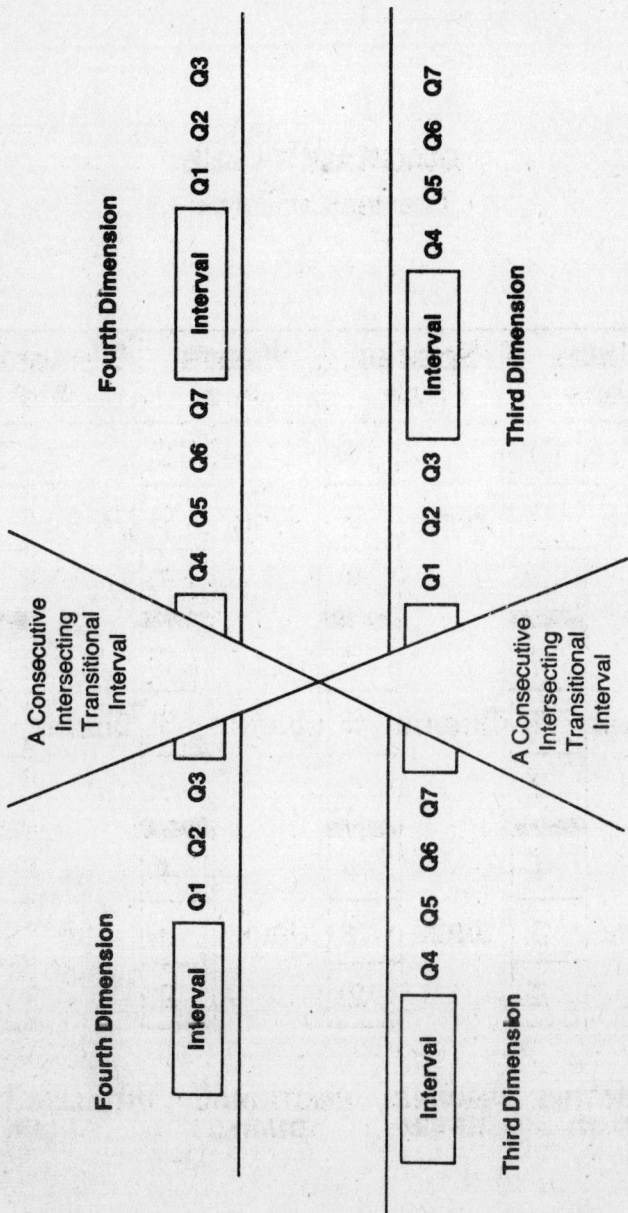

Fourth Dimension

Interval | Q1 Q2 Q3

A Consecutive Intersecting Transitional Interval

Q4 Q5 Q6 Q7 | Interval

Fourth Dimension

Third Dimension

Interval | Q1 Q2 Q3

A Consecutive Intersecting Transitional Interval

Q4 Q5 Q6 Q7 | Interval

Third Dimension

DIAGRAM THREE
The deck of Cards

Clubs Ace		Spades Ace		Hearts Ace		Diamonds Ace	
	10		10		10		10
King	9	King	9	King	9	King	9
	8		8		8		8
	7		7		7		7
Queen	6	Queen	6	Queen	6	Queen	6
	5		5		5		5
	4		4		4		4
Jack	3	Jack	3	Jack	3	Jack	3
	2		2		2		2

INSTINCTIVE BRAIN	MOVING BRAIN	EMOTIONAL BRAIN	INTELLECTUAL BRAIN

(Diagram Four)
The Suit of Diamonds
(The Intellectual Brain)
Ace of Diamonds
(The Unifier)

(K) The king of diamonds represents the Intellectual part of the Intellectual brain.

(10) Within the king, the ten of diamonds represents the Intellectual part of the Intellectual part, of the Intellectual brain.

(9) The nine of diamonds represents the Emotional part of the Intellectual part of the Intellectual brain.

(8) The Eight of diamonds represents the Moving or Instinctive part of the Intellectual part of the Intellectual brain.

(Q) The queen of diamonds represents the Emotional part of the Intellectual brain.

(7) Within the queen, the seven of diamonds represents the Intellectual part of the Emotional part of the Intellectual brain.

(6) The six of diamonds represents the Emotional part of the Emotional part of the Intellectual brain.

(5) The five of diamonds represents the Moving or Instinctive part of the Emotional part of the Intellectual brain.

(J) The jack of diamonds represents the Moving or Instinctive part of the Intellectual brain.

(4) Within the jack, the four of diamonds represents the Intellectual part of the Moving or Instinctive part of the Intellectual brain.

(3) The three of diamonds represents the Emotional part of the Moving or Instinctive part of the Intellectual brain.

(2) The Two of diamonds represents the Moving or Instinctive part of the Moving or Instinctive part of the Intellectual brain.

The jokers represent the first two divisions of the soul.

(Diagram Five)
The Suit of Hearts
(The Emotional Brain)
Ace of Hearts
(The Unifier)

(K)   The king of hearts represents the Intellectual part of the Emotional brain.

(10) Within the king, the ten of hearts represents the Intellectual part of the Intellectual part of the Emotional brain.

(9)   The nine of hearts represents the Emotional part of the Intellectual part of the Emotional brain.

(8)   The eight of hearts represents the Moving or Instinctive part of the Intellectual part of the Emotional brain.

(Q)   The queen of hearts represents the Emotional part of the Emotional brain.

(7)   Within the queen, the seven of hearts represents the Intellectual part of the Emotional part of the Emotional brain.

(6)   The six of hearts represents the Emotional part of the Emotional part of the Emotional brain.

(5)   The five of hearts represents the Moving or Instinctive part of the Emotional part of the Emotional brain.

(J)   The jack of hearts represents the Moving or Instinctive part of the Emotional brain.

(4)   Within the jack, the four of hearts represents the Intellectual part of the Moving or Instinctive part of the Emotional brain.

(3)   The three of hearts represents the Emotional part of the Moving or Instinctive part of the Emotional brain.

(2)   The two of hearts represents the Moving or Instinctive part of the Moving or Instinctive part of the Emotional brain.

The jokers represent the first two divisions of the soul.

33

(Diagram Six)

The Suit of Spades
(The Moving Brain)
Ace of Spades
(The Unifier)

(K) The king of spades represents the Intellectual part of the Moving brain.

(10) Within the king, the ten of spades represents the Intellectual part of the Intellectual part of the Moving brain.

(9) The nine of spades represent the Emotional part of the Intellectual part of the Moving brain.

(8) The eight of spades represents the Moving or Instinctive part of the Intellectual part of the Moving brain.

(Q) The queen of spades represents the Emotional part of the Moving brain.

(7) Within the queen, the seven of spades represents the Intellectual part of the Emotional part of the Moving brain.

(6) The six of spades represents the Emotional part of the Emotional part of the Moving brain.

(5) The five of spades represents the Moving or Instinctive part of the Emotional part of the Moving brain.

(J) The jack of Spades represents the Moving or Instinctive part of the Moving brain.

(4) Within the jack, the four of spades represents the Intellectual part of the Moving or Instinctive part of the Moving brain.

(3) The three of spades represents the Emotional part of the Moving or Instinctive part of the Moving brain.

(2) The two of spades represents the Moving or Instinctive part of the Moving or Instinctive part of the Moving brain.

The jokers represent the first two divisions of the soul.

(Diagram Seven)
The Suit of Clubs
(The Instinctive Brain)
Ace of Clubs
(The Unifier)

(K)   The king of clubs represents the Intellectual part of the Instinctive brain.

(10)   Within the king, the ten of clubs represents the Intellectual part of the Intellectual part of the Instinctive brain.

(9)   The nine of clubs represents the Emotional part of the Intellectual part of the Instinctive brain.

(8)   The eight of clubs represents the Moving or Instinctive part of the Intellectual part of the Instinctive brain.

(Q)   The queen of clubs represents the Emotional part of the Instinctive brain.

(7)   Within the queen, the seven of clubs represents the Intellectual part of the Emotional part of the Instinctive brain.

(6)   The six of clubs represents the Emotional part of the Emotional part of the Instinctive brain.

(5)   The five of clubs represents the Moving or Instinctive part of the Emotional part of the Instinctive brain.

(J)   The jack of clubs represents the Moving or Instinctive part of the Instinctive brain.

(4)   Within the jack, the four of clubs represents the Intellectual part of the Moving or Instinctive part of the Instinctive brain.

(3)   The three of clubs represents the Emotional part of the Moving or Instinctive part of the Instinctive brain.

(2)   The two of clubs represents the Moving or Instinctive part of the Moving or Instinctive part of the Instinctive brain.

The jokers represent the first two divisions of the soul.

In Brief

This book, *The Mechanics of God: A Theory on the Transition of Species and Events,* is a seminal work, one which will see many years of change. In this first treatment I have listed some aspects of those laws which I feel are most essential to understanding what Man is, and what he can become.

The laws of Body Type, Alchemy, Features and Essence are also very important, yet I must refrain in this edition from giving them their proper due. I did wish you to know about them and to give you a general idea of their meaning.

Body Types: There are seven body types: the Mercurial, Saturn, Martial, Jovial, Lunar, Venusian and Solar. They are fixed in motion on what is called the enneagram. They are governed by the spheres from which they receive their names. The saturnine type is an active-positive type, the martial an active-negative type, the jovial a passive-positive type, the lunar a passive-negative type, the venusian a passive-positive type, the mercurial an active-negative type, the solar an active-positive type. All people, all species and events are subject to typing; are responsive to the influence of the spheres.*

Alchemy: There are four degrees of alchemy: Gold, Silver, Copper and Lead. Gold is the finest, lead the least fine. All people, animals, countries, homes, cars, all species and events have an alchemy—a degree of refinement or coarseness. Much of what we like or dislike stems from alchemical preferences and prejudices.

* (See *Body Types* by Joel Friedlander, Globe Press, N.Y.)

Features: In every human being there is a built-in flaw, a tragic tendency. Saturnine types are subject to dominance; martials are subject to destructiveness and power; jovials to power and/or vanity; lunars to wilfulness and lunacy; venusians to non-existence; mercurials are subject to power and vanity; and the solar to power, naivete and vanity. Along with these features, which are related to type, are the non-related features to which all types are subject. These are fear, tramp, greed and self-pity (see page 103)

Essence: All species and events have an individual and hereditary core, an essential fluid that relates to all their parts. This foundation of relativity between parts is called essence. Man's greatest successes can be had only with the help of this foundation because it remains a constant resource where many other characteristics of man can deviate or mutate. Essence too can mutate but this is rare.

Examples:

England's prime minister, Margaret Thatcher is a martial type with a gold alchemy, a feature of power and a northern essence. Her success as prime minister is due to the fact that the English are a saturnine nation. For the saturnine type to gain new strengths it must move toward that type on the enneagram just ahead of it. The martial type is just ahead of the saturn. This places Margaret Thatcher in the perfect position to lead. The overcautious, distant, rule-oriented English need to risk the possible suffering of embarrassment caused by acting more spontaneously.

Gorbachev is a jovial-lunar, his country is a jovial-lunar country. Jovials are positive-passive types, lunars passive-negative. Gorbachev has both these aspects, thus he feels more directly the needs of the people. Previous leaders were not in harmony with the national type. The jovial is often a generous, socially relaxed type which has an ease and attraction that can harmonize an environment. If Gorbachev fails to better the lives of the Russian people it will be due to the wilfulness of the lunar type in the people. Wilfulness of the lunar will resist change even when it is good.

Ronald Reagan is a saturn-mars type. He is centred in the Moving part of the Emotional brain, his chief feature is dominance, his alchemy gold. Nancy is a solar type. America is a saturn–mars nation. The relationship between Reagan and the American nation had to be good because the country and its leader were of the same type and centre of gravity.

George Bush is a lunar-venusian type. For him to understand the nation will be more difficult. Lunars are a stubborn, meek and secretive type that choose the isolation of routine over confrontation and change. Venusians tend to non-exist. People around Bush will need to understand the aggressive saturn-mars nation for him.

Tyson and Givens are opposing active-negative types. Tyson martial and Givens mercurial. A union between these two types must include tremendous conflict and in most cases, if there is marriage, there will be divorce.

India is a solar-lunar-venusian country with a copper-lead alchemy. France is mercurial with a feature of vanity. The Italians are venusian mercurials centred in the Emotional brain. The Germans are martial with the features of power and destructiveness.

All studies and research being done in science, psychology, medicine, diet, class, child behaviour, etc., without the knowledge of type, feature, brain centre, alchemy and essence, will be incomplete. Take diet, or the efforts being made to find the right combination of people for long distance space travel. Certainly if you put martial and mercurial types together in a closed environment for an extended period of time they could kill each other. They are both active-negative types. The jovial and venusian types and those centred in the Emotional brain are all subject to cellular bulk (fatness), and weight fluctuation. For them to lose weight permanently is almost impossible. Diet programmes put together by people centred in the Moving brain are not suitable to these types. The jovial (Santa Claus) is the least capable of all the types when it comes to weight loss.

More examples:

Elizabeth Taylor is a venusian-mercury with a silver alchemy and a feature of vanity. Woody Allen is a lunar with lunatic. Mia Farrow a solar-lunar. Abraham Lincoln was a pure saturn with dominance. Pure types are not common, most people are a combination. The

German Shepherd dog is a saturn-mars dog. The piranha a martial fish, the blue jay a mercury-saturn bird, the bear a jovial-lunar, the eagle a saturn-mars, the hawk martial, the crane saturn, the humming bird, monkey and the hyena mercury. People frequently buy a dog of the same type that they are themselves.

Charlton Heston is a saturn-mars with a gold alchemy and a feature of dominance. Dustin Hoffman a venusian-mercury, Queen Elizabeth II a lunar with a gold alchemy and a feature of wilfulness. Prince Charles is centred in the Instinctive part of the Moving brain, with a silver alchemy, his body type is lunar-venusian. Diana is a solar-saturn with a gold alchemy, Sarah is a mars-jovial, Andrew a mercury-solar. Prince Philip is a saturn type with a chief feature of non-existence. Mitterrand of France is a mercury.

The barrel cactus is a mars-jovial plant, the weeping willow a venusian tree. The knotty pine martial, swamps lunar-venusian, desert martial. The Matterhorn saturn-mars, Ayer's Rock in Australia mars-jovial.

The implication in typing species and events is that at the moment of conception of a species or event influences passing from those spheres which were most prominent at conception contribute very much to the habit and character of that which is born. Then differences between species and events are not an expression of individuality. There is no individual personality in mind when types are cast.

"The unexamined life is not worth living"

SOCRATES

A

ACCIDENT

We call something accidental when we have little knowledge or understanding of why it happened.

*****

ACTION

As what I do now, in the present, enters the past and has an effect on the future, in the same way what I do now as it enters the future has an effect on the past.

*****

AGEING

The very familiar process of ageing could not take place if the law of seven had not entered the third dimension. Other laws were at work as well, but the law of seven established the rhythms of life and death. How strange, though, that something so small as a baby chick could not become a chicken without the help of something so large as the law of seven.

*****

ANIMALS

Animals, reptiles, birds and insects can detect a coming earthquake, storm or catastrophe by their heightened sensitivity to the emanations of recurring future memory coming from the fourth dimension. And we step on the bugs, skin the reptiles, pluck the birds and butcher the animals.

*****

Our assumption that micro-organisms, plants and animals exist without the capacity for contemplation of the divine is to assert that our concept of divinity is the only one there is. We do some harm to plants and animals when we kill and eat them; yet, our assumption that they are not intelligent enough to contemplate, is a greater injury.

*****

Believing ours to be the highest order of intelligence—a belief which might be humbled only by the arrival of beings from another planet—is most unwise.

*****

Do animals pray, do they feel guilt?

*****

Man regards animals as less divine than he, because they appear to him to be dumb. Yet man, when taken as a receiver and transmitter for influences of the fourth dimension, may well be less capable of conducting those influences than animals.

*****

ART

In today's art market novelty and style are more marketable than professionalism. Professionalism and mastery of subject matter and materials should not be sacrificed for the market. Popular art is possible without professionalism, but great art is not.

*****

Most of modern art is a crime waiting to be discovered.

*****

Critics are often little more than the waste product of talent.

*****

Surrealism deals with unreal realism. Dimensional illustration examines the abstractions of reality.

*****

A person who looks extreme and acts extreme may be just that, but that does not make him an artist.

• *****

It was a great idea to abstract form, but the idea has been used to popularize all manner of base novelty rather than to give people new concepts.

*****

It was a sad day in the history of man when Picasso popularized mediocrity.

*****

Great art is the result when several series guided by the mind of a master, meet at their respective Q7-Q1 intervals in a consecutive intersecting interval and pass that consecutive intersecting interval to form one recurring series which we call a work of art.

*****

Abstract art was often the best that the ancients could do. For modern man it is often the worst.

*****

In the absence of a professional spontaneity and inspiration; the fuels of creative expression, simply explode or slither into the meaningless menageries of amateurism.

*****

As an almost endless source of giving great realism provides us with
hidden details in the obvious. The more giving art is the greater it is.

*****

Put quite simply—he is not an artist who can not draw any more than
he is a musician who cannot· play an instrument, or he a pilot who can
not fly a plane. Any man with a knife is not called a surgeon.

*****

ASTROLOGY

The stars have a greater influence on the four-dimensional body of man
than they do upon his three-dimensional body. In the past, masters of
astrology, through seeing man as the stars see him, understood the
evolutionary relationship between the four-dimensional body of man and
his three-dimensional one. Then predictions of an individual's future and
behavioural analysis were seen in relation to what a man, as a whole,
could become, not as it is practised today where he is regarded only
three dimensionally as a part. In our age body type information is nearer
to the truth three-dimensionally.

*****

In the past astrology was a sharp tool precise enough to enlighten the
individual. Today, it has been reduced to a socially accepted
generalization.

*****

The starlit sky of deep space is seen by the naked eye as two-dimensional.
Astrological signs were implemented to correct this weakness by
suggesting three-dimensional forms with four-dimensional time bodies.

*****

Because man himself has so small an effect on the causes of his actions
astrology must be taken into consideration.

*****

How often do astrologers of today actually look at the stars?

*****

ATTENTION

The focus of attention gives that upon which the attention is focused influence over that which has given the focus. For an individual to protect himself, to prevent the identity of his attention from being taken, he must give his attention to an awareness of himself. Without this giving of attention to one's self, attention and identity are not one's own. For example— the Pope has the attention of the Christian world focused on him. This attention focused on him gives him control over the identity of the people. If they diid not give him their attention he could not control them. Any well-known athlete, actress, president, religious fanatic etc., are a point of focus, therefore a source of influence. Give your attention to a hamburger and a hamburger controls you; give it to love, pain, anger, and they control you. Give it to a book and the book controls you. Give it to an awareness of yourself where you are, doing what you are doing and you control yourself, you decide the fate of your identity.

*****

How often do we leave our bodies unattended? That is, when we give our attention only to something we are thinking about doing, or seeing, or something in the past or future, we are not aware of what our body is doing in the present. Were we to die in one of these unattended moments our own death would pass unnoticed by us.

*****

When we bring the focus of our attention to the present moment, to where we are, doing what we are doing, we place ourselves in a position where the fourth dimension has influence over us through our will to make it so. This ascension by volition into the fourth dimension is commonly called enlightenment.

*****

Directing our attention to an awareness of ourselves in the present helps us to reclaim the trail of energy that we leave behind us moment by moment.

*****

If, for example, you could have an awareness of yourself with your attention focused on a single object, a candle flame, and not lose that point of focus of attention by thinking of other things, imagining other things, seeing other things, then in the awareness of your single focus of attention you would begin to acquire a view of the fourth-dimensional body of that same candle flame—to see that candle under different laws.

*****

One way of gaining strength for controlling attention is to reduce the tendency of being vague, of permitting our thoughts and feelings to just drift along. We must choose to be specific, notice details, doubt the foundations of opinion, question the source of our values, keep our mind silent while someone else is speaking. Ask if we know the facts about a given subject—do we really understand what was said? Can we see individuals in a crowd, specific leaves on a tree, see the details of a face, hear the different instruments in a song?

*****

Normally our focus of attention is on only one thing: a subject outside ourselves—the weather, where we are driving to, someone we are talking to, or on something inside ourselves— a past memory of someone we love, planning for the future, imaginings, expectations, etc.

*****

Attention is active, that upon which it is focused is passive, and an awareness of both is neutral. Were the awareness active or passive it would be dualistic and non-evolutionary.

*****

In an effort to control attention we can see clearly that something stops us, that we deviate and the awareness of our attention is lost. The ability to control attention requires an awareness of the impending approach of the interval.

*****

Give your attention to an awareness of your attention.

*****

When we feel no imposition on us by time and space—our attention is simultaneously in the fourth, third and second dimensions.

*****

Attention is not a question of concentration, it is one of focus.

*****

Successful control of attention must not be relegated to the three-dimensional ego that we call 'I'. To say that 'I' am locating and directing my attention is to lose the awareness of attention. The awareness of attention is neutral and this neutrality leads to the activization of the observer.

*****

We cannot locate attention without first seeing that we do not know where it is. To know oneself means to know what the identity of one's attention is. Most people think they know themselves and that it follows that they must also have an awareness of where their attention is. But if you were to stop anyone walking on the street and ask him if he was aware of where his attention was a couple of seconds ago, after stopping to think, he would say that he was not; your asking if he was aware would make him more aware in the moment that you asked but not before.

*****

To hold and direct attention while in the interval, forces man to assume the responsibilities for the continuation of the series. Generally we defer this great opportunity to some God or saint.

*****

The laws that govern all societies, religions, governments, require that those societies, religions, governments have a focus of attention. The identity of the individuals upon which society focuses its attention is irrelevant. Celebrities are needed as celebrities, not as individuals.

*****

My aim is to focus my attention on myself sitting here, in this room, at this moment because this is where I am, and what I am doing.

*****

Pleasure and pain are both methods of focusing attention. We know where our attention is when we are experiencing pleasure or pain. The like and dislike of pleasure and pain is less important than the fact that our attention is visible.

*****

The attention that you use to concentrate on reading, on listening, on eating, playing, loving can be used to control matter in a molecular state before it is defined by form.

*****

Attention is a delicate and fragile thing. It is strong enough to penetrate the realms of the fourth dimension yet easily lost here and now by numerous distractions. Even as we read this thought, focus is slipping away from us. Everything distracts us. There is nothing in the environment that supports our effort. You are alone where you are. I am alone where I am.

*****

Were we to take a hundred people and stand them twenty feet apart all along a shore, each would say that the beam of sunlight he sees comes directly to him. That all one hundred people see a beam of sunlight implies that the sun shines equally, not personally, across the entire body of water in front of the shore.

*****

The illusion that we are unique is made possible in part by that weakness in the eye that sees us as the focal point of perspective, casts over our psyche the distinct feeling that everything is focused on us and must be taken personally. The weather, the time of day, the having of babies, jobs, desires, there is nothing personal in any of this, yet we persist moment by moment on thinking that there is. Life is not personal, death is not personal, god is not personal.

Our taking of things personally permits us to justify all manner of human weakness, from the most severe expressions of anger, envy and jealousy, to the most subtle forms of criticisms and judgments. To gain that inner strength necessary for the creation of awareness of attention, we must attempt wherever possible to reduce this taking of things personally, and its resulting permission of the expression of vice.

*****

To verify the law of attention we must begin again with the question, 'Where is my attention now? Is it on myself sitting here in this place with an awareness of what I am doing? Or is it off in some imagination or distant memory?' This question must be asked over and over, again and again. But there are many obstacles in making this effort. Most frequently the first obstacle is 'Why do it?' It is not an occupation, no one is going to pay you for it. Or give you a pat on the back if you succeed. And it can be a lot of trouble because at first it confuses you by interrupting your normal level of competence.

*****

It is very important for us to know the tolerances of our attention span: for how long and upon what subjects are we able to hold attention. For example—an intellectually centred person will be able to hold an acute level of attention on the study of quantum theory for ten minutes where an instinctively centred person will begin to lose interest after two minutes. We should know any time that we give our attention to something exactly when that attention begins to fade. To continue reading while attention is distracted from reading means that what we are reading is being forgotten as soon as we read it. An awareness of when attention fades helps to reduce the necessity of repeating many things.

*****

The knowledge of laws is objective knowledge, knowledge which has not been created by man. To use this knowledge as a catalyst to help locate and control attention can lead to objective observation, to seeing man as the laws see him.

*****

Basically the attention that we give to things is the same attention we must give to an awareness of ourselves as we are seeing things, doing things, thinking things. For example, as you are reading these words, you want to be as aware of yourself reading as much as you are aware of what you are reading. That is, you and where you are, should not be absent in the attention that you give to what you are reading, thinking, feeling, seeing, etc.

*****

That the focus of attention causes in us a chemical reaction is observable when we take the example of a good food advertisement that makes us salivate, or the description of an injury that makes us sick, or the thought of a loved one that makes us happy or sad.

*****

Human attention, when it is focused for long periods of time on the present, places man—as an instrument—into his own hands. With this tool he can measure the force of the fourth dimension as it enters the third. An eventual and necessary step that man must take if he wishes to examine and verify immortality.

*****

Directed attention is the great key to human development.

*****

Our attention is generally loosely fitted around something we call 'I'. Giving our attention to more than one part of ourselves at the same time tends to reduce this error by increasing awareness. Increase in awareness is more of an identity than what we call 'I'. The problem is that this awareness of attention is not human so we tend to overlook its great importance.

*****

That upon which we focus our attention becomes what we consider to be life's greatest value. This is why it is so important for us to know where our attention is and what it is doing. If we don't know where it is and what it is doing we have no way of evaluating for ourselves what is and is not of value.

*****

We have only one attention, but that one attention can be given to more than one thing—can be enlarged to such a size that the known limits of the universe by comparison would seem small.

*****

We were born with attention, but not with the ability to direct attention. Controlling, directing, and dividing attention must be learned.

*****

Attention is not an idea, it is an action.

*****

To control and direct attention toward an awareness of ourselves in the present gives us the strength we need to transform the raw energies of gravity, emanations, electromagnetism, radio waves, thoughts, time, etc., which are passing through us at this moment.

*****

Body type, alchemy and brain center refer to the car, attention refers to the driver. Where we direct our attention, where the driver chooses to go, is our choice, and it is the only choice we have.

*****

AWARENESS

We are quite simply not aware of ourselves at the same moment that we are aware of things which are not ourselves.

*****

Awareness of yourself in the present takes the whole of what you are, whereas thinking that you are in the present only involves a mental image of yourself.

B

BEHAVIOUR

A principle problem with our understanding human behaviour is that we first do not understand what is a human being.

*****

When we act the way we assume others wish us to act, we expect them to act according to our wishes.

*****

'Living in the now' is an often misunderstood idea which leads to irresponsibility toward the future and failure to learn from the past.

*****

A schizophrenic is a psychological Siamese twins. Cutting off one of the heads is not a cure.

*****

Someone in search of spirituality does not have the same needs as a troubled or disturbed person, yet both may seek help from the same source.

*****

Much of our hostility towards other people comes from one person being in the quantas of a series while another is in an interval. When this is the case, communication is difficult and misunderstandings prevail.

*****

The many varied responses of man can be attributed to alchemy, features, the five brains, brain centre or centre of gravity, body type, essence and personality. Of course there are influences other than these. Yet much of what we observe; the great verity of behavioral characteristics, mannerisms, attitudes, feelings, instinctive and emotional responses, speeds of reaction time, learning ability, capacities, strengths, weaknesses, etc. are the result of a momentary, fluctuating or continued predominance of one or more degrees of intelligence acting out its influence on the human being. Man is not a singular, he is a multiple; a complex meeting place for the pronouncement of life.

For example, let us take the person of Miss Heather Hollyfield. She is a saturn-solar type with a chief feature of vanity. She has a gold alchemy and is centred in the higher part of the emotional brain, (the King of Hearts). Her essence is well developed and her personality weak.

Each condition of her human being is intelligent; alchemy has its own intelligence, chief feature has its own intelligence, body type has its own intelligence and so on. All these diverse processes are united in and by the physical human body, which is like having many drivers and only one car. And the car has only one driver's seat; so there are times of conflict because each driver is trying to outsmart the others for the right to drive. Thus Miss Hollyfield will sometimes be outgoing and naively cheerful in response to having her solar parts in the driver's seat. At other times she will be overly proud, too full of the image of herself; she will look down on the faults of others as if she has no faults. This is her vanity in the driver's seat. At yet another time her mood will be very warm emotionally yet distant and thoughtful. Here the King of Hearts is driving. Then in a flash of disapproval she will reprimand her son for making a slight smudge on her spotless glass table; her gold alchemy has taken the wheel. In each case the reasoning is different, yet the person remains Heather Hollyfield. And so it is with each of us, our Dr. Jekyll and Mr. Hyde are a family with numerous relatives more than they are a duo.

*****

Manipulation is not creative. Therefore a manipulative man is going to control people but not give to them.

*****

With every clear realization that we have about our own and other people's behaviour, there are many more hidden and inaccurate conclusions that we have made which we are not aware of.

*****

The very personal view that we have of ourselves and the world in which we live, comes from the various combinations of the impersonal laws which we have identified with.

For example:

— A Saturn with the chief feature of dominance will see the world quite differently than a Mercury with vanity. Neither is one's view more right than the other, and neither is responsible for the tendencies of his type and feature.

— Verification of the laws which act upon the behaviour of man, can help us to accept the diversity of opinion which we regularly criticize rather than understand.

*****

In every form of addiction we find that the bearer of the addiction feels confident that he can convince others of his and their need for his addiction.

*****

First generalize behavior, then find in the generalities that which is specific to you.

*****

Someone who feels no internal need to correct external manifestations of his weaknesses will necessarily doubt that he has weaknesses.

*****

Judgement is a form of attachment which binds our attention to what we judge.

*****

Love and affection are spontaneous and unorganized and as such have less value in families and societies where order, promptness, efficiency and cleanliness are most important.

*****

A criminal sees the victim as the cause of his crime.

*****

The more unhappy a person is with himself the greater his need to control other people.

*****

The character of a strong man is seen in how he uses his strength, not in his having strength.

*****

Most relationship failure is due to the intellectual part of the instinctive centre thinking that secrecy is the key to instinctive well being. When we become intimate with another person our instinctive centre's boundaries are threatened as some being other than our own instinctive centre begins to know things about us that we ourselves are not aware of. Once the instinctive centre realizes that intimacy has cost it its secrecy it becomes very defensive and arguments follow. And the man, because men are more instinctive than women, out of fear of the greater emotional perceptivity of women, usually defends himself with some type of instinctive: physical, reaction like walking out, refusing to talk about the problem or even hitting the woman.

*****

BELIEF

Most people are not secure in their beliefs unless they share those beliefs within the support structure of a group. Thus, most of what is called 'My Faith,' is merely the expression of group identity.

*****

Belief is simply not necessary as a means of supporting hope of a life after death.

Any form of belief implies judgement.

*****

How can we think that what we believe is not an illusion when we think that what other people believe is?

*****

Belief generally instructs a person to think himself to be a better person than those who do not share his belief.

*****

Believe in yourself more than all Christians believe in Christ, more than all Buddhists believe in Buddha, more than all Muslims believe in Muhammad.

*****

Religious groups require that belief in that group's tenets be made dependent upon the activities and attitudes of the group. Thus dependence and belief are made into one. And it would be more honest to say, 'I am dependent,' than to say, 'I believe.'

*****

Must we disbelieve others to believe in ourselves?

*****

Belief in itself does not provide for the truth.

*****

Even if the God that man has imagined exists, belief in that God would reduce man's ability to learn about and understand God. Unfortunately belief, once it has taken hold of a person, tends to prevent further questioning and the subsequent learning which arises from questioning.

*****

Judge a man not by what he believes but by how he acts upon his beliefs.

*****

BIBLE

The animals of Noah's Ark were not animals and Noah was not a man. The story being told in the Bible refers to laws and substances not animals and people. Noah plus one man and one woman represent the law of three.

*****

There has not been, nor is there, nor will there be, a last judgment. Once past the inaccurate interpretations of world doom, man will move more quickly to his greater purpose. The dawn of the twenty first century will represent the beginning of his awareness of that purpose.

*****

Jesus of Nazareth will never return to this earth. His job is done.

*****

The Bible was not written to be understood.

*****

BIG BANG

At all locations in time and space where the fourth dimension penetrates the third, there is registered on that time or space an intense explosion. The magnitude of that explosion will be known by how great an effect the produced species or event has on the environment within which it was created. The Big Bang, though only a small part of the process of creation, does give—because of its enormous effect—a good visual diagram of the creative power held in the interval when that interval is filled by forces of the fourth dimension.

*****

The big bang theory, though wonderfully inventive, is basically an attempt by man to reduce the vast and invisible origin of matter to that primitive reason known as human logic.

*****

There is no more permanence in the big bang theory than there is in a world record for the shot put.

BIRTH

A baby despairs on leaving the womb because while in the womb it experienced the materiality of the body without the burden of gravity. All the efforts and imaginings of man that aim at freeing him from gravity are essentially degrees of the foetus's longing to return to the womb. In the womb man is nearer to god.

*****

BLACK HOLES

A species or event entering an interval can exit that interval unchanged if it has retained enough of its original identity while in the interval. The same is true for a proton or any other particle entering a 'black hole'. If that proton or a particle can retain its original proton or particle state while in the black hole it will at some point exit unchanged. Future observations will show that this can and does happen.

*****

We have found the body, or at least a part of the body of our universe, and where they is a body there must also be a means of feeding that body. This is the unacknowledged logic behind our search for black holes. If black holes don't exist as a function which helps to feed and create the body of the universe, something else does. Also we have no way of knowing if it was a black hole rather than a big bang that got the universe going.

*****

The power than runs a black hole is based on the process of transformation

of that which enters it. Transformation of even the smallest species or
event generates intense energies because the activation of a transformation
releases the energy contained within the process of transformation. And
the process of transformation is nourished by its own expression.

*****

To a certain extent the human mouth and stomach are a phenomenon
synonymous with that of the black hole. The energy which we exert after
a meal is proportionately equal to that energy exerted by a black hole
after it eats. Black holes do more than run quasars. They conflict
psychologically with galaxies. Just as humans do more than play baseball
and read newspapers.

*****

A black hole is to a galaxy what an interval is to a series.

*****

BODY

Were we to avoid cutting our hair, finger- and toe-nails for the whole
of our life we would see how much energy our body radiates in the form
of matter and we would look a lot like a plant with roots.

*****

Our five senses remain sharp and our minds dull because of eating and
our need to eat.

*****

Out-of-body experiences are a brief transference of the identity of one's
attention in the third dimension to that of the identity of one's attention
in the fourth dimension. In the fourth dimension identity is achieved by
giving attention to what observes; whereas in the third dimension identity
is achieved by giving attention to what is being observed.

*****

BRAINS

The four brains: Each of the four brains in man has its own rate of digestion of experience and its own understanding of the significance of that experience. The rate of digestion can be seen as the process which creates the velocity of reaction. The Intellectual brain has the lowest rate of digestion, the lowest velocity. This means that the world as seen by the Intellectual brain is processed much more slowly than the world as seen by the other three brains. For example—I'm walking over a bridge. I glance at an old lady standing on the bridge. In the time of that one glance I see the history of that lady, that she has suffered and is bitter, that the world is meaningless to her. It's not that I know every fact of her life but that in some way I can see the whole of the result of her life—all in that one glance. This is the world of the Emotional brain. The Instinctive brain in the same glance might notice how warmly she is dressed or if her position on the bridge is dangerous. The Moving brain would think: 'Has she stopped, is she about to walk on, will I bump into her?' The Intellectual brain might wonder what her name is. There is a great difference between seeing the life of a person and wondering what his or her name is. Also the pre-established functions of a brain contribute to the different rates of comprehension between brains. For example— the Emotional brain comprehends the full meaning of a stranger's glance in an instant but is very slow with understanding calculus. The Intellectual brain, whose purpose is to understand calculus, would take less time even though it is a slower brain.

*****

The greater part of man's brain was designed to facilitate the creation of matter and the transformation of heavy matter into degrees of molecularity and spirit. With so little real interest in spirit it is not surprising that just a mere six to ten per cent of our brain is in use.

*****

Science is built primarily out of the legitimate needs of the Intellectual brain, religion out of the legitimate needs of the Emotional brain. These two forces in society will remain in conflict so long as man fails to realize that the differences between the two make them equal not opposite.

*****

When we apply the blueprint of the five brains, as illustrated by the deck of cards, to the concept of multiple intersecting intervals, we begin to establish a visual image' of the processes which actualize human manifestations (See diagram three.) Also we can see how complex even the simplest manifestation can be. A full understanding of the human being would require a present awareness of the multiple intersecting intervals which take place between the five brains, types, alchemy, feature, and essence. A four-dimensional being is necessary for a complete awareness of the three-dimensional being.

*****

The function of any brain is to process, organize and assimilate the information of its experience for the purpose of coordinating the processes of that brain's body with the brain itself. The five brains of man function in this manner separately in relation to their own centres and collectively in relation to the body of the total human being.

*****

The growth of the human brain, in being dependent upon experiences of the human body, will grow in proportion to those experiences.

*****

The difference between a perception of yourself and a sense of yourself, is that the perception is emotional and the sense instinctive.

*****

The Moving brain is the most passive of the five brains.

*****

The three brains in man which make memory of the future possible are the Unifier, the Instinctive and the Emotional brains. The Unifier clarifies perception, the Instinctive and Emotional form understanding. Perception and understanding taken together generate a realization of future memory. To a certain extent the Instinctive brain is the past of future memory and the Emotional brain the future.

*****

Each human being is centred in one of the four brains: The Intellectual, Moving, Instinctive, and Emotional. (No one is centred in the Unifier.) To be centred in a brain means that one's orientation to the world is either Intellectual—logical; Moving—spatial; Instinctive—sensory; or Emotional—perceptual. An intellectually centred person will judge the activities and tendencies of the Emotional, Moving and Instinctive brains as being less real than thought, concepts and ideas. The Emotional brain will judge thinking, sensing and moving activities as less real than feelings. The Moving brain sees feeling, sensing and thinking as less real than doing things. And the Instinctive brain sees the sensory world as more real than the world of thought, feelings and doing. Why one person is outraged by the misue of words, another by the misuse of feelings, another by neglect of the senses and another by the absence of moving activity is made clear when we understand the differences between the four brains.

*****

Each of the five brains age at different speeds, and are born into the body at different times. In this regard man has five ages. The first is Instinctive, followed by the Moving; then by the Intellectual, then by the Emotional which is the most ageless of the four. The Unifier is the last to be born and the first to shut down.

*****

Perception precedes thought, is greater than thought.

*****

The Emotional brain in harmony with the Unifier produces the clearest and deepest perceptions. Women, in being more emotional than men are often more perceptive. Men can benefit enormously from the perceptivity of women, but they often do not because they rarely respect this form of intelligence.

*****

Understanding which brain we are centred in can help with estimating which occupation we are best suited for. Intellectual types are well suited to office work and certain types of programming. Lunars are also suitable for these jobs. Moving and Instinctive types are good at dance and most sports. Emotional types are good at jobs that deal with personal relations such as social work, preaching, and marriage counselling. We are not going to find a Queen of Hearts type on the stage doing classical ballet in any situation other than a comedy, nor are we going to find an Intellectual type vying for a heavyweight boxing match.

Most people are Moving and/or Instinctive types, so most jobs can be done by these types. Emotional and Intellectual types are frequently forced to work in areas better suited to the Moving and Instinctive types. Imbalance in society, similar to that imbalance in nature which over-breeds rats, insects, diseases, etc. is a result of an overabundance of one or two types. A balanced society would be one in which the Intellectual, Emotional, Moving and Instinctive needs of that society were given equal respect and satisfaction. The fifty or so years which represented the golden age of ancient Greece was one such period in the history of man. At present we have an imbalance of Moving and Instinctive types which forces upon our budding international society a kind of material greed based on fears and insecurities natural to the Instinctive brain.

*****

The proper and full development of the Unifier will provide man with the function of his sixth sense.

*****

The awareness and the subsequent discomfort that comes when someone walks up behind us or stares at us comes from the Intellectual part of the Instinctive centre; the king of clubs.

*****

The act of sizing a person up is primarily an instinctive centre function.

*****

C

CHARACTER

Much of what is false in man is a result of his sacrificing three-dimensional values for two-dimensional values—depth for the surface appearance.

*****

When you are ill which do you wish most, sympathy or healing?

*****

Nothing unites the many differences in man more completely than his sense of discovery. Discovery precedes fear, greed, hate, love, devotion, habit, all the defined reactions that we as individuals assume to be characteristics of our individuality. Children live in a state of discovery and they usually get along fine with each other until definitions of character are handed down to them by adults.

*****

Where some people identify themselves and their safety in the environment by making friends, others make enemies.

*****

What we have become as a result of the modifications we have made to our character by absorbing the opinions that others have of us can be called our false character, our false personality. What we have been given at birth can be called our essence. And what we have earned can be called our true character, our true personality.

*****

Leadership does not corrupt character so often as character corrupts leadership.

*****

A powerful character assumes no need to explain its actions.

*****

CHILDREN

Children and babies are often more capable of entering the fourth dimension than adults, but they are less capable of understanding its importance. Adults must regain the innocence and the wonder that they had as children, while retaining the lessons of their experience.

*****

An adult who molests a child does so for the pleasure of experiencing perversion without restraint, as the innocence of a child cannot yet define insult to its dignity. In this adults prove that desire can be added to basic evil.

*****

Children are not to be shown pictures of a man and woman making love because we don't want our children to become immoral or lustful, but it is okay to show them pictures of death camps, assassinations, murders and war because we don't mind them becoming more prejudiced bitter and hateful. Then we must conclude that immorality and lust are held to be of greater evil than murder and hatefulness.

*****

When you look into the eyes of a one-to two-hour-old baby what you see in those eyes is something that the baby will forget before he learns to talk. This forgetting of the child is the greatest loss we share as a human race. For, while in the darkness of the womb, the foetus has seen the origin of light.

Very young children, because of their greater freedom from habit, are nearer than adults to the fourth dimension. If they could tell us what they see, know for themselves what they see, we would all be a lot wiser.

*****

CHRIST

To have the knowledge of laws and an ability to control the effect of those laws, is a greater miracle than an act of walking on water or raising the dead. Christ could not have been too impressed by his own miracles.

*****

COINCIDENCE

When the timing of events in our lives appears to be guided by some supernatural hand responding directly to our personal wishes, we get this feeling of 'I am special'. We must beware, as most of these experiences are the natural consequence of the interaction of laws. This does not exclude those moments wherein a Carrier has acted. But it does make it clear that in either case we should not run off gleefully patting ourselves on the back.

*****

CREATION

The unexpected arrival in one's mind of a new thought, one which penetrates the whole of one's body and life, is that same spark arriving from the fourth dimension which ignited the creation of our little universe.

*****

D

DARWIN

Any theory pertaining to the world of matter that does not calculate the invisible in which matter is suspended must necessarily fall short of the truth.

*****

I can tell you that Darwin is wrong. I have seen that he is wrong, but this is not your proof.

*****

Man is not just a biological creature born of biological change. Were this so no thought of the non-biological state of enlightenment could enter his mind.

*****

Darwin's visualization of the process of evolution is quite simply, too logical.

*****

DEATH

We do not die in the past or the future. When we die we die only in the present. The degree to which we live our lives in the past or the future is the degree to which we are unprepared for that moment in the present when we die.

*****

Death too was born, had an origin, a birth place.

*****

Dying brings one closer to god only if we allow our being of fewer possibilities to be consumed, eaten, by a being of greater possibilities. There can be no increase of possibilities without the consumption of lesser possibilities by the greater—no life without death.

Our fear of death is fear of being devoured and the fear of being devoured by beings of fewer possibilities. We cover that fear with religious songs, symbols, habits and beliefs.

To be consumed by a being of greater possibilities is not bad but it is the end of our three-dimensional human identity.

*****

The body is dying—a daily awareness of this fact makes one Self-Religious as nothing in life is closer to oneself than one's own death. And nothing is more guaranteed nor more motivating than the realization of how little time we have, before we die, to accomplish even the most basic level of spiritual goodness.

*****

People do not know themselves when they die because they are not in the habit of dying.

*****

When we increase our awareness of incoming events to a present speed equal to that of the speed of light, a common event, such as taking a bite of food, becomes a strikingly mystical experience.

We know that a bite of food, as it gets closer to our mouth, begins to disappear from our sight. Normally this is taken to be a simple and unexceptional act. But when observed at the speed of light, the motion of one's hand bringing food to the mouth is slowed to minus 186,000 miles per second; thus we see in profound slow motion an action which we commonly regard as only so much trivia.

Usually we are aware in a very general way of the flow of events rather than the moment of life and death of each event; its arrival and disappearance. It is a great shock for us to realize how blind we are to the disappearance of one moment into the next. We think death comes only at dying, when in fact at the passing of each moment there is a disappearance of things seen that is so great, that death itself disappears by comparison.

*****

There can only be a life after death to the degree that there is life before death.

*****

At the time of death a saint does not give his attention to the death of the physical body, rather he gives it to an awareness of the death of the body. And the awareness of death outlives dying.

*****

It is amazing how great man's desire is to stop change, to regiment, to formalize, to standardize, to create a life without intervals. Death of the body represents a change in the degree of possibilities, whereas the death of change means the absence of possibilities. The death of change is the death we should fear.

*****

That the law of seven exists in this dimension and in the fourth dimension is proof that there is life after the death of the three-dimensional body— life which does not necessitate human form.

*****

DIMENSIONS

Man lives in three dimensions—the second, third and fourth. Yet he believes that only his three-dimensional world is reality. A five-brained being living in three dimensions certainly cannot have just one definition of reality, life after death, and evolution.

*****

Two qualities of life which give a false sense of security to beings of the third dimension are habit and expectation. Habit generates a body of associations that create the illusion of continuous unity; and expectations produce a view of the future that assures us that life will remain continuous.

*****

If we take a freeway filled with fast moving cars and observe it from a hill, we can see that there is little possibility of halting the flow of traffic without there being an accident. The second dimension is like the freeway. In the third dimension there are intersections on this freeway, therefore more chances for things to change. In the fourth dimension we have left the freeway and entered the city where there are intersections every block, therefore even more possibilities for change.

*****

How would a thing look to us if it were without gravity, without light, could not be touched or smelled, if it had no history, no form?

*****

The second, third and fourth dimensions can be taken as differences in intensity and refinement of forces. We cannot be certain of the exact ratio of their differences, but we can know through observation that the intensity of force rises with each higher dimension.

*****

The fourth dimension has a greater influence upon the third than the third does upon itself.

*****

To see the third dimension as it is governed by those laws which govern the fourth is to be in the fourth. And how wonderful it is to see this world apart from being in it. And, too, how beautiful it is.

*****

The third dimension is not eliminated by the presence of the fourth. It is included in the presence of the fourth.

*****

An awareness of the whole of a body in the fourth dimension exists at any moment in the fourth dimension, thus any time that a four-dimensional body enters the third dimension it will contain the entire force of the whole of its body as it exists in the fourth dimension.

*****

In the world of mathematics, dimensions are given the characteristic properties of length, area and volume. A two dimensional world is that which has an area yet no volume. A three-dimensional world is one that has volume. TV, in being two-dimensional, gives people primarily shallow non-volume two- dimensional experiences. Thus, from the consumption of, say, two hours of TV time you get two minutes of three-dimensional value, not a particularly good buy.

*****

We are quite simply underwater in the third dimension, looking up at the sky (the fourth dimension), which we can see only as a blur.

*****

Most forms of social morality are the result of three dimensional species degenerating into the second dimension.

*****

We define the third dimension more by its limitations than by its strengths.

*****

Photographs reduce three-dimensional form to two dimensions. This is why some religions fear photos.

*****

To better understand the third dimension as it is governed by those laws that govern the fourth, we can take the picture of a scene—the scene itself—and the lifetime of that scene, and visualize all three as existing, one on top of the other, in the same moment.

*****

Where in the third dimension, we have broken lines of activity, in the fourth there are interconnecting circles and spirals of infinite growth and infinite degeneration.

*****

Dimension shock can be quite similar to culture shock in that a three-dimensional being, upon entering the fourth, finds himself in an unfamiliar land where the people and customs are far different from his own. There is something familiar and unfamiliar at the same time.

*****

Though we have assumed several methods of describing and measuring dimensions, we have not yet found a means whereby we can calculate exactly when one dimension merges with another; when a line becomes a plain, a plain a cube, a cube a body of time. Rough estimates can be made by stating that higher dimensions contain greater possibilities of enlightenment, and lower dimensions have fewer possibilities.

*****

A full minute in the fourth dimension would change our relationship to everything.

*****

Perspective in the third dimension employs a single point of focus, everything seen in perspective comes from and goes to the point of focus. Perspective in the fourth dimension has no single point of focus.

*****

The lower the dimension the greater the distance between moments of memory and clarity of memory.

*****

With the exception of out of body experiences we only see our face two dimensionally.

*****

The present continues to be the present in the fourth dimension where in the third dimension each present diminishes into the past and the future.

*****

There is neither absolute time nor absolute space because reality, in having more than one dimension, expresses a difference in time and space with each change of dimension. For man to understand the strengths and limitations of his reality he must first understand which dimension or dimensions make up his reality.

DIMENSIONAL ILLUSTRATIONS

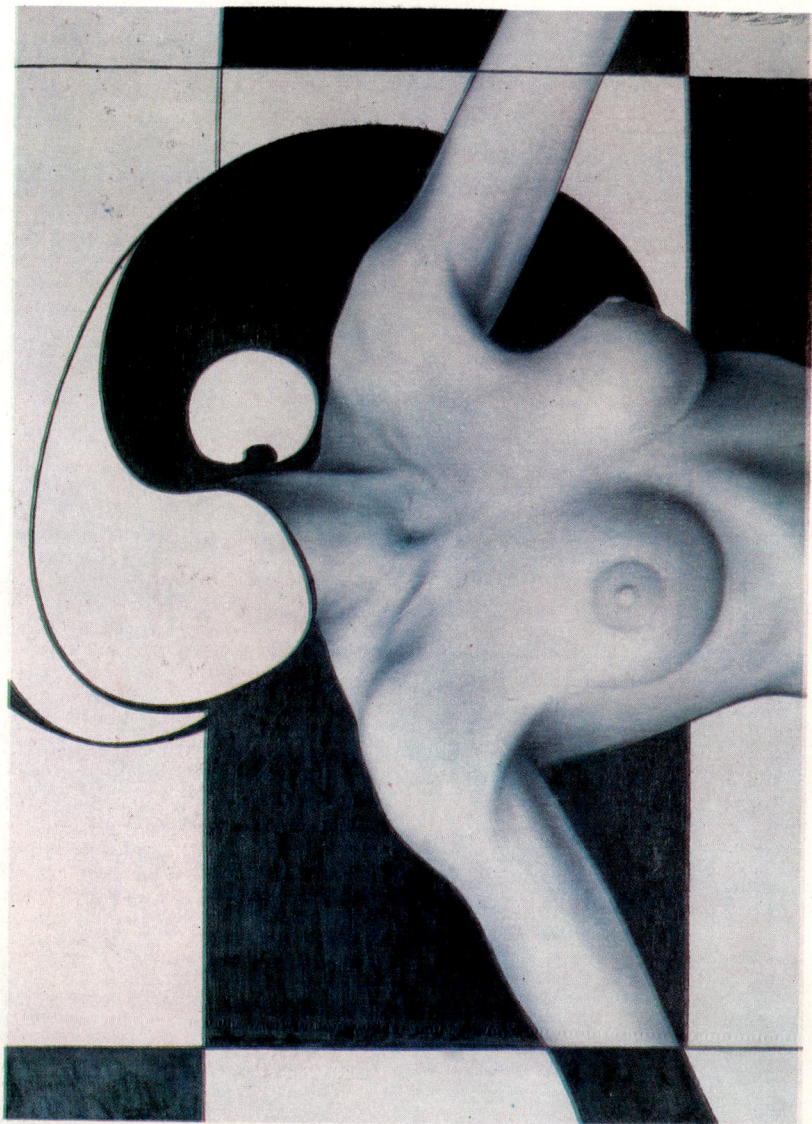

A Two-Dimensional Head on a Three-Dimensional Body

The Image of a Feeling

Four Body Parts in One Motion

The Wives of Adam

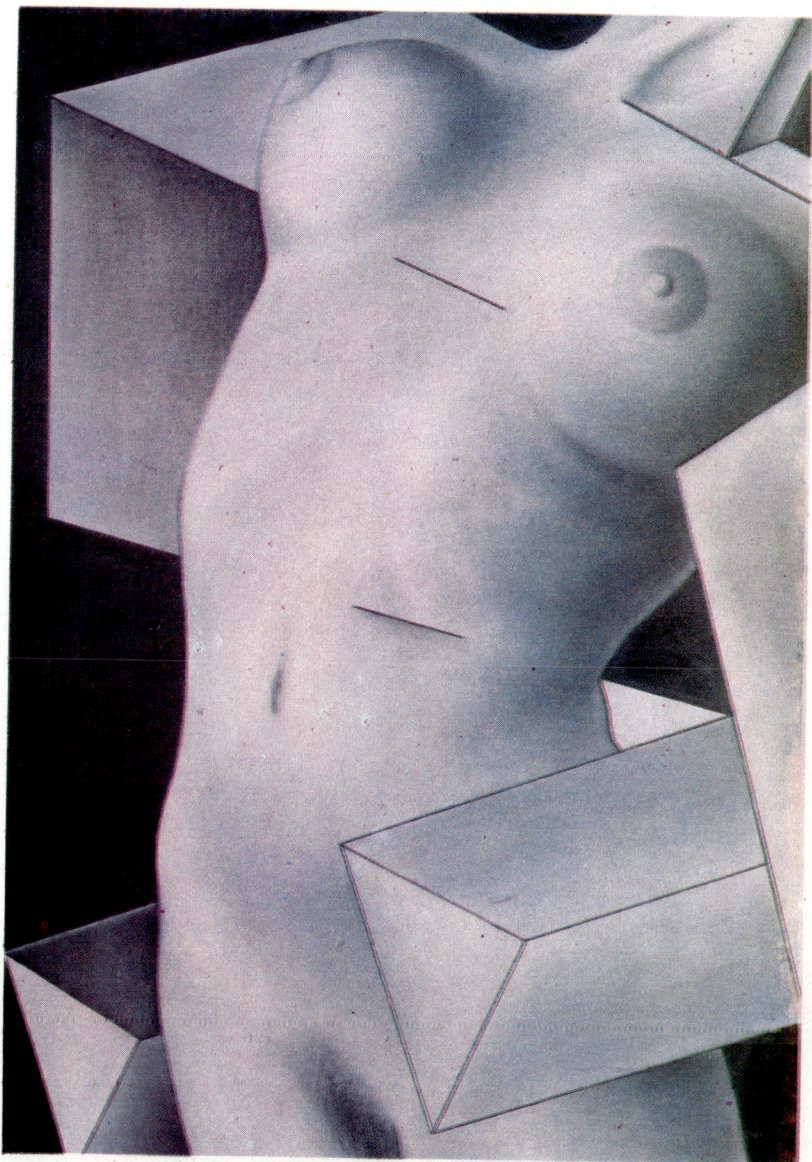

Three Dimensions Descending into Two

Innocence Feeding the World

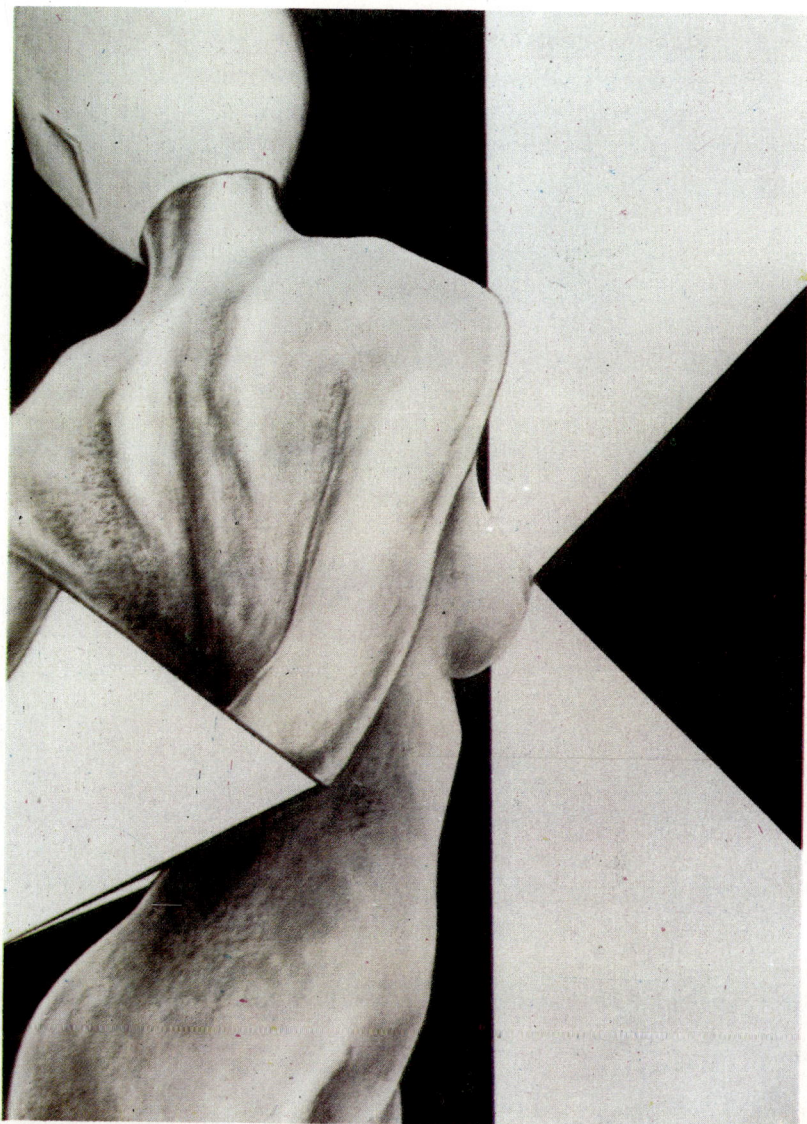

Equally Front and Back

An Invasion of Conscience

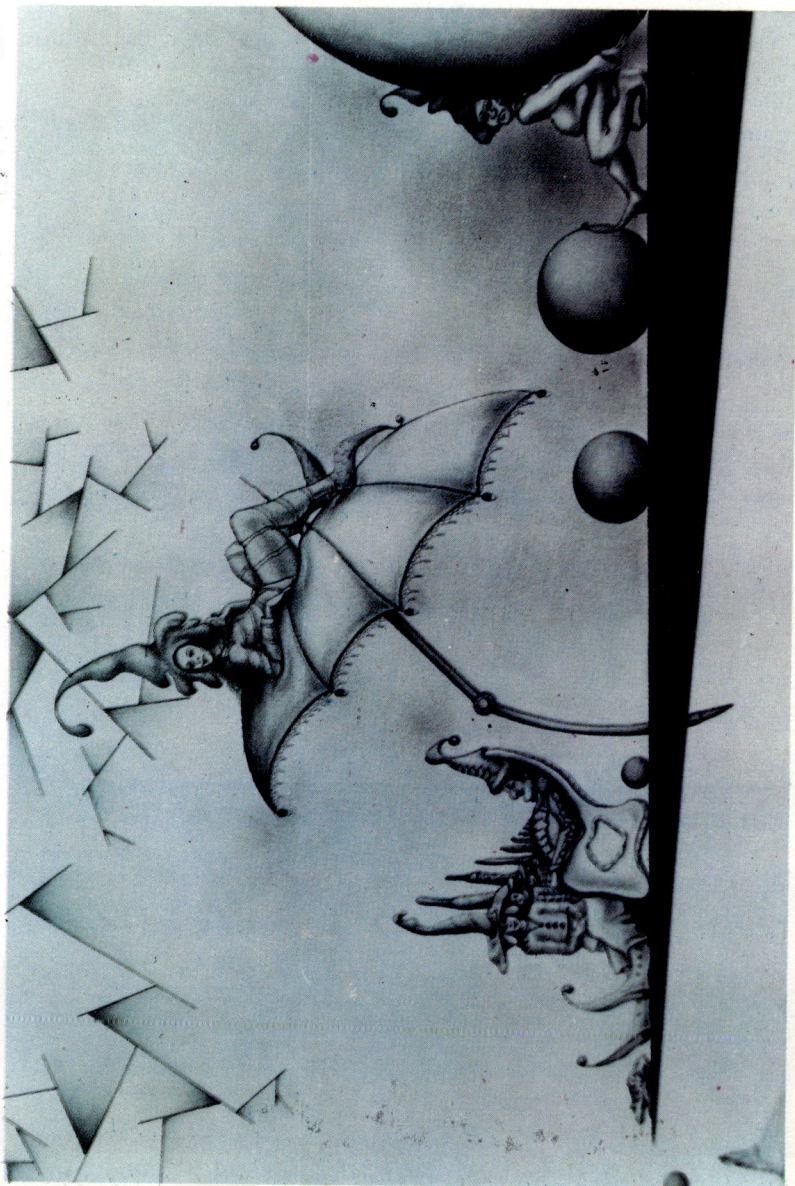

Neglecting Reason

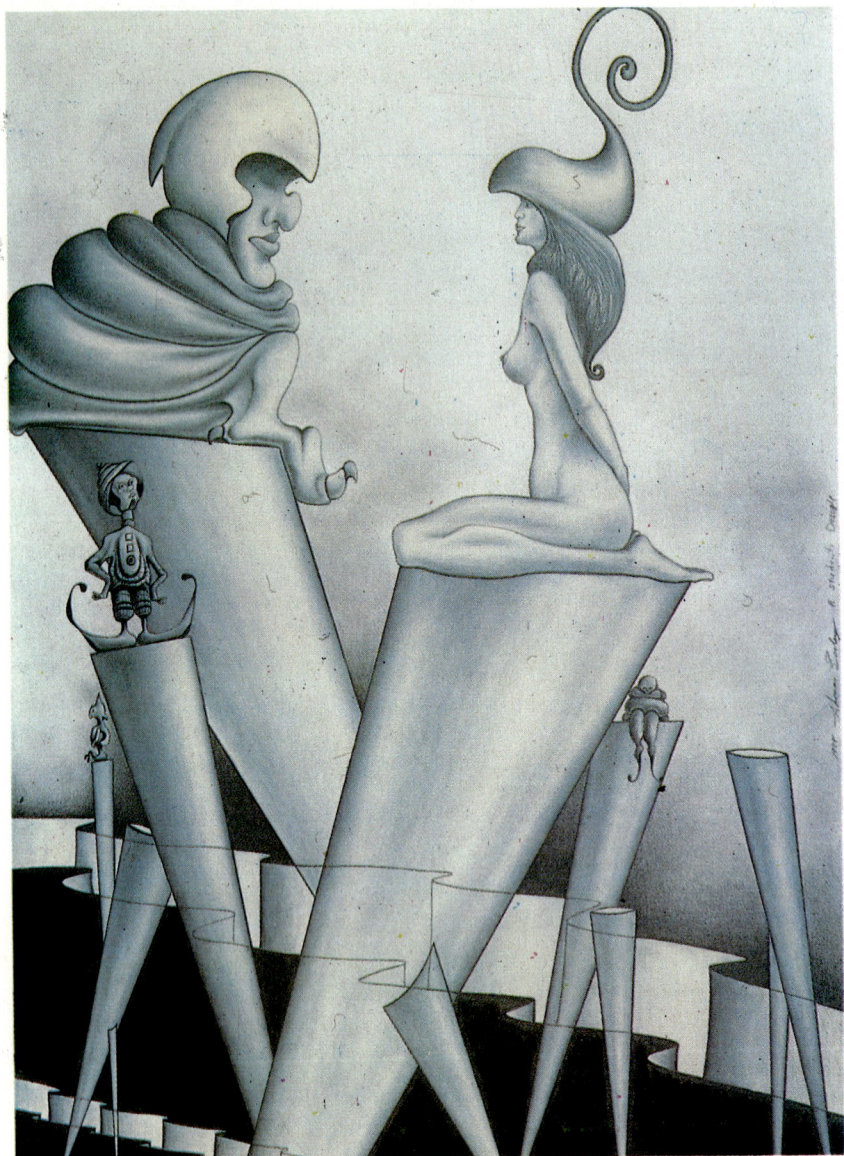

A Student's Disciple

A Question of Learning

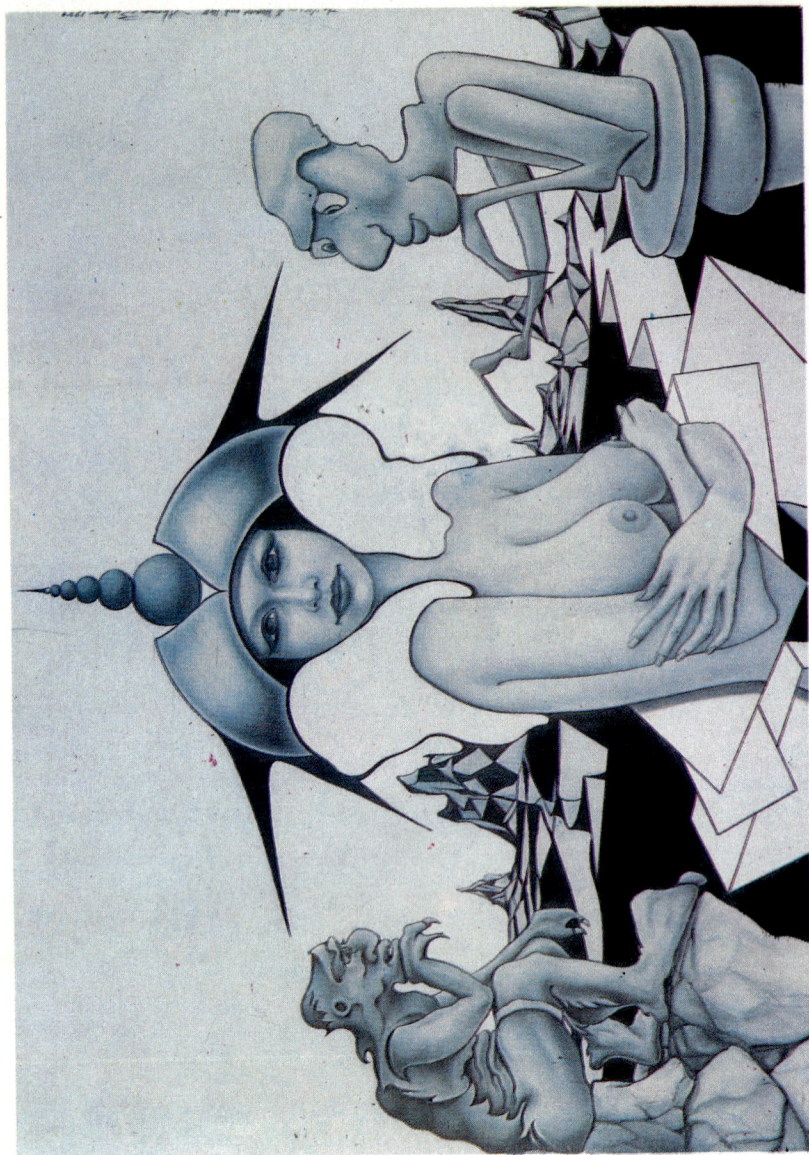

The Virgin of Heaven and Hell

Dreams of Forgiving

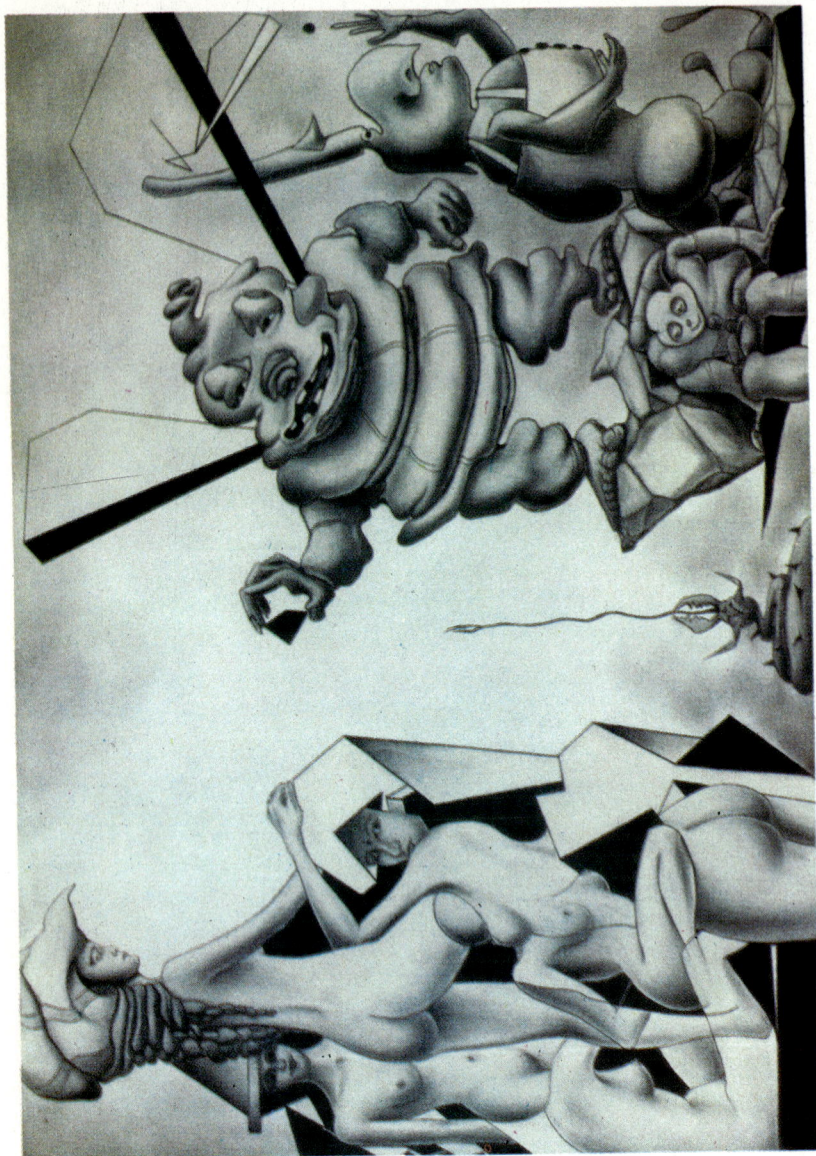

The Angel of Peace of Mind

Sweet Dreams

The Long Way Home

DISTRACTIONS

The interval is the principal point where distraction occurs. It is important to remember this because when you decide to focus your attention on the present many distractions from within the interval will rise up to stop you. Most distractions come from imaginings about the future or imaginings associated to memory from the past. All forms of meditation are aimed at concentrating attention on the present by reducing distraction, and by gaining control over the interval where the distraction takes place.

*****

DRAMA

Striking contrast contains an element of the unexpected which produces drama. Violence is more often shocking than it is dramatic.

*****

Drama is the act of revealing contradictions.

*****

DREAMS

Most realizations of dreaming are a result of unresolved problems from the day overlapping into the night.

*****

The images in dreams are manufactured by the Moving brain. The sensations of strangulation, heat, pleasure, fear, etc., come from the Instinctive brain. Expressions of despair, rejection, caring, injustice, etc., come from the Emotional brain. Dialogue comes from the Intellectual brain and the degree of vibrance comes from the Unifier. Also sexually stimulating dreams are influenced by the Unifier.

*****

Dreams are, in a sense, like the heartbeat of the brain, and like the heart dreams laboriously pound away whether we notice them or not.

*****

Dreams flow through our heads all day and all night, just like radio waves flow through houses. And like radio waves which can be picked up by a radio, dreams are picked up by our awareness of them.

*****

Dreaming is influenced by the position of the head. Lying on the back of the head, the left or right side of the head produces in each case a difference in the nature of the dream. And that difference is often related to a greater or lesser sense of well being in the dream.

*****

Our most profound dreams are memories.

*****

Our standing upright in dreams comes from daytime memory.

*****

Where are the eyes that see dreams and whose eyes are they? Dreams are a form of perception and perception is in itself sight and the light to see.

*****

DRUGS

Impressions—thoughts—feelings—emanations, things that man sees, all produce a chemical reaction in him as they enter his body. Love at first sight is a good example of this. Drugs can change a person's chemistry, open his eyes to the strangeness of other worlds. Drugs can open the door to the fourth dimension and they can close it if abused. Most of what we know about drugs is the abuse of them.

*****

Many drugs break down the illusions of three-dimensional reality. That is why we fear them, for what would our society be without its illusions?

That drugs destroy the body is not as much to fear as the destruction of illusions.

*****

E

EMANATIONS

Emanations are an ultra-fine state of matter.

*****

We know that people emanate certain desires, feelings, thoughts. And in general we assume that those emanations stop with us when we receive them. But they don't stop with us, rather they continue through us, through the past and future and into deep space.

*****

Emanations are a stimulus in the same way that radio waves stimulate, or the sight of blood stimulates, or sunlight and darkness stimulate.

*****

Emanations serve as fuel to transport the wishes of four-dimensional beings.

*****

The moon has a chemical influence on man that comes more from its emanations, than from its gravitational pull.

*****

Emanations are a form of speech, a means of communication. To say that emanations do not exist, or that their existence is insignificant because we cannot measure or understand the language, is erroneous.

*****

A fully developed human being is going to receive a greater number of emanations at a greater depth of penetration than will an undeveloped human being. Reading emanations, for a master of the language, is like reading a book.

*****

ENERGY

The essential requirement for entering the fourth dimension is concentrated fine energy, energy finer and faster than a particle of light. Human beings have been designed to produce that energy.

*****

ENLIGHTENMENT

A single virus within the body of a man can multiply and destroy the man, so too can an enlightened man, if he is followed by thousands of enlightened men, multiply and destroy the body of the solar system. The shock of mass enlightenment within the solar system would weaken the necessary illusion of its fragile three dimensional shell too much. The solar system is simply not prepared for such a shock, nor is the species of man evolved enough to be that shocking. This is partially the reason why possibilities of enlightenment are highly regulated; why followers are in greater numbers than leaders; why it is so difficult for us to bring our attention to an awareness of ourselves in the present and to keep it there. All beings that evolve toward a more enlightened state of existence must pay for that evolution by breaking through the shell of their illusions. The solar system and the universe are in the process of creating their illusions, they are embryonic and well protected from the possibility of a wave of enlightened beings rushing at them from the earth.

*****

The pathway to heaven need not be littered with confusing terminology, symbols, rituals, forms, group dependence and fear. A consistent effort to be aware of oneself where one is while doing what one is doing, not only lights the way, it is the way.

*****

Enlightenment is not given, only the tools are given.

*****

Any genuine step toward the spiritual must take one into the interval. This is often a confusing and disorienting experience, where it becomes difficult to measure the difference between illusion and reality.

*****

ESOTERIC

Understanding of esotericism is determined not by the accumulation of esoteric ideas, but by the application of those ideas.

*****

ETERNITY

People who cannot live without rules cannot live in eternity. Orthodox Jews, fundamentalist Christians and Muslims are too formalized, too rule-oriented. Obedience to rule is a false interpretation of that harmony which is necessary for the human being to expand into eternity. Rules are not harmony; they are the shackles of ignorance.

*****

EUPHORIA

Euphoria is that state in man resulting from the unified action of at least three of man's five brains. When all five work in harmony man thinks he is indestructible. Such feelings are generally infrequent as it is quite rare for the five brains to behave so well.

*****

EVE

In the early days of man, the intervals in the developing mind of man were so small that choice was not possible. Once the first interval enlarged, and choice was made possible, Eve was born. Eve was the creation of choice, not the creation of woman.

*****

EVIL

One of the greatest errors in considering the nature of other dimensions is to assume that if they give us pain, they are evil.

*****

Fear of pain causes us to misunderstand evil. True evil is the conscious and premeditated act of reducing possibilities of enlightenment.

*****

There are strong degenerative forces in all dimensions that exist as the effort made by a lower dimension to suck into itself those beings and laws of the dimension above it. The devil, for man, is just this process in the second dimension. The success of this force can crystallize man in fixed, inflexible beliefs, attitudes and illusions, the contradiction of which often results in negative confrontations, such as witch burning, the justification of religious wars, etc.

*****

Evil is that venom in us which justifies our own weaknesses by projecting those weaknesses on to others.

*****

History has proven that many more people have been horribly treated, tortured and killed in the name of God than in the name of Satan.

How strange that we blame Satan for evils that befall us and kill in the name of God. Obviously there is something very wrong with our thinking on this subject.

*****

EVOLUTION

What we observe as the evolution of man and the universe takes place in accordance with the manifestations of the law of seven. That the universe evolves in a particular pattern comes from the regular and expected order of the first three and last four quantas, that the universe evolves at random comes from the unpredictable and often explosive intervals.

*****

The evolution of man (when taken to mean that process wherein matter is transformed into spirit), becomes a question of the actualization of greater or lesser possibilities. That is, evolution, rather than being the linear process of adaptation is a complex warring between species and events for the privilege of receiving greater possibilities. The acquiring of greater possibilities is an increase in evolutionary values, and the loss of possibilities the degeneration of evolutionary values. A principal error in Darwin's concept of evolution is its singularity, and the supposition that through adaptation things change from what they are into something that they are not. There is not just one evolution of man. The human being is a complex five brain-being—a creature of five centres superimposed one upon another, not just one body with one brain and only one possible evolution. Given the knowledge of these five brains and the necessary observation of their functioning, it becomes verifiably clear that the evolution of man cannot be known by the categorizing and collecting of bones and bits of habitat.

*****

Organic chemicals, inanimate matter, anti-matter, and other as yet undiscovered particles were first produced by the conflict between laws of the second, third, and fourth dimensions. The creation of form, or what we recognize as life, both human and otherwise, was determined by whatever force it was that acted most decidedly on those chemicals, matters and particles while they were suspended in the void of the interval. That force which was most decisive could have been anything from laws of the second dimension to carriers of the fourth.

*****

The origin of man is not a secret that is being kept from us, it is an experience that we are either not able to face or simply not able to remember. Were it possible for someone to enter the four-dimensional body of mankind he would have access to the past and future of the race. We could then ask him what happened, where did we come from, are we really descendants of the ape, are we from another planet, were we handcrafted by the gods. As it stands now, mankind remembers nothing of its birth—just as a child emerging from the womb into the shock of daylight and perspective remembers nothing of that experience. A great shock was required to place the human species on this earth.

*****

Although evolution cannot occur without change, change is not evolution.

*****

Transformation changes a thing from what it is to what it is not. With adaptation the essential nature of a species or event remains the same.

*****

Creative forces of the fourth dimension act on the material three-dimensional world through intervals in material being. The interval, upon receipt of fourth-dimensional forces of creation becomes itself a source of creation, a source not so powerful as the original: something like moonlight as opposed to the purer sunlight that it reflects.

*****

So when did the ape, that proposed predecessor of the human race change over to the violent, problematic, thinking man? And why is the ape still around? As the parent of man he should have died long ago. It is more likely that we came with the ape rather than from him.

*****

EXERCISES

Here are a number of very simple exercises which can help to prepare you for dimension shock:
1.   When watching TV and film try to see, at the same time that

you watch the action, the man and the crew behind the camera.

2. When you look at a photo, try to see yourself looking at the photo at the same time that you look at the photo.

3. Imagine yourself pursuing someone at the same time that someone is pursuing you.

4. While in your room in your house in your country, try to remember that there are other rooms, other homes, other countries all of which exist at the same time.

5. Observe that your attention, your awareness of things goes from subject to subject without your choosing the subjects that attract it.

6. Maintain an awareness of your whole body rather than just a part of it.

7. Remain aware of the fact that when you speak you listen at the same time.

8. When looking at a clock try to realize that different times are the same moment, and that it is the same time somewhere billions of light years away.

9. Remember that with all things there are degrees—different depths of water, densities of stone, brilliance of thought—degrees of understanding, varying heights of mountains—degrees of truth, intelligence, learning.

10. Remember when you walk that you can walk faster or slower, that you have a choice to walk faster or slower.

11. Avoid giving too much attention to frustration and impatience.

12. Try to feel the earth turning, and remember that we are floating in space. The changing light of day, the moving shadows, and sunset all speak of the earth turning.

13. First become aware of how many and diversified the thoughts are which run around inside your head. Then try to stop the thoughts and study the awareness.

14. Try to lie to yourself intentionally.

15. Respect silence.

16. Don't forget yourself when you are remembering other people.

17. Think that you can think differently, then find something to think differently about.

18. Try to hold your attention on yourself physically and at the same time on the reflection of yourself as you stand in front of a mirror. Our tendency is to give our attention to one or the other; to the reflection or to ourselves standing there.

19. Try to remember that this is the last time you will be in this moment—this moment right now—right now where you are doing

what you are doing—this is the last time that circumstances will allow this moment to occur in this way—then there is the next moment—the one here now—and then the next and the next and the next.

20.   Hold out your arm. Entering the fourth dimension is that simple. Staying in the fourth dimension is difficult. Just as it is difficult to keep holding out your arm.

These exercises, and many others, just as simple, help to increase awareness; and this increased awareness generates more energy. A higher level of energy in us makes our connecting to the high energy of the fourth dimension less shocking.

*****

F

FAITH

The only faith one needs, if one needs any faith at all, is that faith of certainty inside oneself that observation and verification of laws can reveal truth.

*****

Can there be faith without dependence upon the subject of faith?

*****

What we know about God and heaven are mere crumbs swept indiscriminately off the table of the fourth dimension. We can know more but not by way of faith. Faith contributes little or nothing to the process of learning.

*****

FAME

Fame does not give a person more to offer. It means that what someone has to offer, be it good or bad, will reach more people.

*****

FEATURE

Dominance, in essence, is a natural ability to engender trust. Vanity, in essence, is a natural ability to find fault. Greed, in essence, is a natural ability to dissatisfy desire. Fear, in essence, is a natural ability to mistrust. Tramp, in essence, is a natural ability to concede. Wilfulness, in essence, is a natural ability to resist. Naivete, in essence, is a natural ability to assume innocence. Lunatic, in essence, is a natural ability to be extreme. Self-pity, in essence is a natural ability to feel concern. Destructiveness, in essence, is a natural ability to challenge. Non-existence, in essence, is a natural ability to conceal. Power, in essence, is a natural ability to intimidate.

None of the characteristics of features are in themselves good or bad. They are an aspect of how people with these features see the world and how other people see them. It is only when a feature develops the negative of reducing possibilities of enlightenment that they are bad.

Also, behavioural patterns related to characteristics in essence are felt to be our most natural, comfortable and most just patterns of behaviour. And we will defend those patterns regardless of what others say.

*****

Our feature is the most frequent architect behind our style of walking.

*****

Vanity is an unhappystate wherein a person expresses self dissatisfaction by finding faults in other people.

*****

Tramp feature has no defense against an attack on self worth.

*****

FILM

Compare the energy level that penetrates our being while we watch a two-dimensional film, with the energy that we receive after the film when we walk into the three-dimensional world of the street outside. Even the best film cannot generate an energy equal to the simplest three-dimensional scene. To a certain extent we could say that a two-dimensional world confronts us, a three dimensional world surrounds us, and a four-dimensional world consumes us.

*****

For a film to succeed as a great film it must pass from the second dimension of the screen into the three-dimensional world of the audience. This can be accomplished by any means that brings the audience into the film, while at the same time reminding them that they are individual parts of an audience sitting in a theatre watching a film.

*****

When any higher dimensional being gives its attention (the identity of its life force) to a lower dimension without retaining its identity in its own dimension, it descends into a world of fewer possibilities. Film should add to our possibilities rather than take away from them; should stop man from giving away his identity rather than encourage him to do so.

*****

The spiritual significance of film has not yet been tapped.

*****

Film, because it can compress and manipulate time, acts as a window to the fourth dimension. If we were able to multiply everything that we see, every object and thing around us by its time body, it would be like running overlapping films of everything that happens in the life of those things. For example, we would see the whole life of a chair, a dog, a window, a toy, etc., revealed before our eyes all at once rather than through the process of time and ageing. You can imagine, with such a concentrated force of energy how much creative power is contained in a moment of the fourth dimension. A moment of the fourth dimension could as easily produce a flower as a sun. Our little nuclear bombs by comparison, are meaningless. We are fascinated by film not because of its subject matter or its ability to tell a story, but because in it we unknowingly detect a hidden power.

*****

FOLLOWERS

Verification of the action of the law of seven can begin to free one from the need to follow, as it will begin to give one the strength to pass intervals on one's own. We are usually attracted to a leader because of his ability to overcome intervals which we cannot overcome ourselves.

*****

A leader does not choose followers so much as followers choose a leader.

*****

To follow requires obedience rather than learning. Learning takes place in the interval, following takes place in the quantas. The law of seven requires that there be a greater number of followers than leaders.

*****

Conflict between followers express the weaknesses of their leaders.

*****

The pretence of followers who claim to have an absolute knowledge of spiritual truths is the most vile form of pretence.

*****

FOOD

Food is that which gives life (energy) by being consumed. It is easy to verify this with the food that we take into our mouths. Not long after we eat, our bodies feel the energy given off in us by what we have eaten. So it is, with what we see, hear, feel, think, etc. All things that come into our body and give energy can be called food. From this we can see that a greater degree of awareness will bring more food into our body and give us more energy. For example, I am sitting here in my chair typing, as I type I attempt to enlarge my degree of awareness by giving attention to my peripheral vision. As this awareness begins to form I add to it the sounds of Eva having a bath. I am holding my attention on this thought and also on the order of thought in what I want to say. All these sources of food are entering the body of my awareness at the same time. I gain energy from this food and transform it into another effort to further enlarge my degree of awareness.

*****

FORM

Religions, governments, and military powers are necessary for the establishment of form. In this necessity they are equal.

*****

Differences in form are much less important than differences in laws which govern form.

*****

FOUR-DIMENSIONAL IMAGES

I knew a man who looked like me when I was you, and nothing could we be.

*****

And she sleeps as a wide open sea, with fishes swimming in her womb.

*****

He said that he was the devil and that the devil was God, not that he was God.

*****

For a while I stood on the edge of life, hearing in my ears, the clown.

*****

Where in the inside of light I have seen some creature being born, and I have seen forms without shadows.

*****

They confessed to dancing in the rain and to laughing with their tears. We were old and they were young, in between the coming years.

*****

Upon that vision of myself I see,
A self that's seeing me.

*****

Higher up in my tree, on my horse,
There was nothing I could do, of course.

*****

FOURTH DIMENSION

Entering the fourth dimension can be achieved by a multiplication of one's awareness. For example, you are sitting in a chair at the dinner table, at first you notice that you are only aware of how hungry you are and that the room is warm. As you begin to concentrate your attention on yourself sitting in that chair in that room you also add an awareness of the sounds on the street and your breathing, then the light in the room, then your feelings about yourself in that room. A further enlargement of your awareness begins to include what you see, touch, remember, smell, think all at the same moment, and within this one moment you begin to lose a sense of time—of a past and a future—as the awareness itself, not the things of which one is aware, exists beyond the limits of time.

And within this new sense of time we also begin to see the reason for being in the things that we are aware of; their past and future are somehow felt by us, felt as an expression of energy. This energy is now visible to us as some kind of life force. The quality of this visibility, what one actually sees, is determined by how long one can sustain this multiplication of awareness. The greater one's ability to sustain awareness of oneself in a place, the greater the penetration into the fourth dimension. The dimension changes by degrees as more awareness is added to the present.

*****

There are several illegitimate approaches to the concentrating of attention that lead to the fourth dimension. The difference between legitimate and illegitimate is the difference between the success of Being and the success of Powers. In human beings, the success of Being is based on the development of the Emotional brain and that brain's relationship to essence. And the success of Powers is based on the development of the Instinctive brain and its relationship to essence. Powers, when taken illegitimately, always include manipulation in a physical way of the environment and of those people in the environment; they take for what they give and sacrifice equals for equals. Being asks for and requires little or nothing from whomever it gives to, as giving in itself nourishes Being. Unconditional love is Being. And the development of Being is a legitimate approach to the fourth dimension.

*****

Four-dimensional stimuli are frequent players in a man's life, yet because he has not learned to recognize them, they appear unfamiliar. The animal in man, that is his instinctive brain, reacts to the unfamiliar with caution, avoidance, fear or violence.

*****

The fourth dimension, in containing the entire lifetime of a species or event, acts upon every moment of the past, present and future of that species or event. This implies that future events are responsible for actions in the past in the same way that past actions are responsible for events in the future.

*****

Once man begins to live in the fourth dimension he will have access to the entire lifetime of the third dimension.

*****

The law of seven, as it is expressed in the fourth dimension, takes on the effect of widening the intervals while shrinking the quantas. Thus, change and diversification of possibilities become more infinite.

*****

Infinity is not a constant in the fourth dimension, it is a greater possibility.

*****

To enter the fourth dimension we must cling to life a little less desperately.

*****

The fourth dimension, compared to the third is like a feast encompassing all tastes compared to a meal of bread and butter. And man, habituated to bread and butter needs time to expand his palate.

*****

If you take all the events that occurred in the life of a public hall and showed them in action all at the same moment, you would have an impression of the fourth dimension, an awareness of the concentration of energy there, and the utter absence of recognizable three-dimensional form.

*****

Regularities are almost non-existent in the fourth dimension: abstraction is the norm.

*****

Just as a magnifying lens, when concentrating moonlight on a piece of paper, doesn't burn a hole in the paper, so too, a lesser being or law of the fourth dimension, when concentrated in the third dimension, doesn't produce much of a shock on the third dimension. This helps to explain the degree of difference in man's experience of the fourth dimension. People like Christ or Buddha were focal points for very strong four-dimensional laws or beings. Most of the time when we lesser beings experience the fourth dimension it is not the great of the fourth dimension that we are in touch with.

*****

Those who say that the fourth dimension has no place in a three-dimensional reality are saying that man can never have a new idea.

*****

The fourth dimension is a real world, a world about which we have little understanding, not a non-world with which we have no relation. Then, it must be obvious to us that a need exists to improve our relationship to that world.

*****

The frontier of the fourth dimension is an expanse beyond imagination, yet within reach.

*****

Carriers of four-dimensional offspring can provide for and carry from one to thousands of foetuses at different stages of development. Human beings of varying lifetimes, as the nourishment for these four-dimensional infants, are looked after and protected by the Carrier, just as we look after cattle or sheep. The concept of a guardian angel comes from what could be called the motherly instinct of the Carrier. Christ is a good example of the transformation of a ninth-life human being into a four-dimensional Carrier capable of supporting many lives of four-dimensional foetuses.

*****

A four-dimensional being is not the fourth dimension itself, though that being is made up of and is subject to the laws of the fourth dimension. We need to be protected by beings of the fourth dimension when that world, with its great impersonal nature, rolls into our fragile little world of the third dimension.

*****

All that we use to guide ourselves as three-dimensional beings in a three-dimensional world is put into question after an experience of the fourth dimension. This is why much preparation is necessary before a person can spend a long period of time in the fourth dimension.

*****

Living in the fourth dimension would be like living in the moment of a conception of thought.

*****

Walking upright is crawling, when viewed from the fourth dimension.

*****

The fourth dimension seems a bit crowded at first because there is so much going on there.

*****

The greater the shock experienced in the third dimension from a fourth-dimensional entry, the greater the length of time that that moment exists in the time body of that which experienced the shock.

*****

Certain types of dreaming come from the fourth dimension unedited because sleep creates an interval in our perceived relationship to reality.

*****

The fourth dimension is the nearest great invisible world in which we can begin to live.

*****

How often do we find life in the third dimension to be unexpected? Certainly the fourth dimension must be more unexpected.

*****

To get a solid image of our time body all we need to do is shoot an hour-long film of ourselves behaving normally, then print each frame of that film on one piece of paper. The image developed by overlapping frames would not appear as that recognizable human being that we call 'I'.

*****

In prolonged space travel the brain will have a greater opportunity to grow, as dependence on the limbs will decrease.

*****

For man to continue on the path to his greatest success he must have an age and a time in which striving to be in the fourth dimension becomes a dominant process in his life.

*****

Like the focus of a magnifying lens which concentrates a large area of sunlight into a fine and energetic spot, a plain cup sitting on a table, when taken as a focus in the third dimension for its time body in the fourth dimension, becomes a source of tremendous energy.

*****

FREUD

What is called a Freudian slip presupposes a knowledge of the origin of an action. Freud was just guessing. He had many good observations, but very little real knowledge.

*****

FUTURE

Life in the solar system and space will pose greater dangers to a man's life than if he were sent naked, blind and unarmed into a dense jungle.

*****

Innocence in the third dimension is indispensable for the survival of the fourth dimension.

*****

In space man will be isolated from the familiarity of the food chain which gives him a sense of order and well-being here on earth. Ants, roaches, flies, moths, etc., are not wanted in space, but something must be there to fill the vacuum.

*****

For our future survival we must develop an ability to understand and retain more than one truth at a time. Generally we get confused and negative when truths appear to contradict each other by arriving at the same interval at the same time.

*****

Man in the distant future will be far more different from man today, than man today is from man of the distant past.

*****

Man in the distant future will experience prolonged periods of time wherein his body will be traveling near to the speed of light. Man of today could not survive this shock because his thoughts are restricted by a rigid three-dimensional definition of reality. Preparing man for space time begins with opening the thought processes to perception without definition. Once the human body arrives at the speed of light, its purpose as a species will be complete and its task in the universe finalized. Beyond the speed of light humanity disintegrates into the lowest levels of the fourth dimension.

*****

At present man creates movement with big explosions which produce little movement; later on he will produce little explosions to make big movement. The latter will follow the discovery of Transition Shock Fuel. Shock fuel is the motivating factor that results from the shock of change. For example, the transition between colours in the colour spectrum is an area in which shock fuel is stored. Thus, a red-sensitive engine, when it passes into blue, would be shock-fuelled by the transition and ignited into further motion. The universe is full of colour, waves of colour—which like waves on the beach have an impact force.

*****

Man in space will be capable of living off the universe in the way that man on earth lives off the land. This new man—this galactic man—will be free of the need for illusions about God. Man is kept from the universe to the degree that he is immersed in his illusions.

*****

Future man will not require the hope of living happily ever after as a solution to present unhappiness, or faith in immortality as an answer to our obvious mortality.

*****

On and near earth man is protected from over-exposure to the highly corrosive emanations of distant and often conflicting spheres and spaces. The first galactic men, men who will venture much beyond earth's protective veneer, can expect to be traumatized by the prolongation in their minds of utterly inexplicable thoughts, some of which can melt skin, stop the heart, or freeze metal. At that time thinking in itself will become an action not the precursor of an action. And carelessness of thought then, as with carelessness of body motion now, will prove fatal.

*****

Beauty on earth is mostly defenceless against man's ruthless appreciation, neglect or intolerance of it. Space and the void are infinitely more beautiful and much more difficult for man to destroy.

*****

Man in space will return to the origin of man on earth as those presently unknown conditions which provide for human life on earth will provide as well for human life in space. Then we will know how great a creator of our race the fourth dimension is.

*****

Rape and murder are primitive forms of communication. Man will always be attracted to this level in his past as long as his future is dominated by gravity.

*****

Gravity repulsion engines use gravity to repulse gravity. In a sense they turn gravity against itself like a mirror reflecting light back to light.

*****

G

GOD

Man's excessive vanity and addiction to power are at the centre of all abuses and misconceptions of god.

*****

How inappropriate a lie it has been to take all the powers and mysteries of the unknown and give them one name, God, and to say I know God and God knows me. Why has such a myth lasted so long and persuaded so many to close their minds and give up their lives?

*****

No one man or woman has been or will be, the word of God on earth, as certainly if there is a god, he must not be so insubstantial a being that mere mortals are required to express and validate his wishes.

*****

As long as people of the world vary in their interpretations of God, we must doubt man's overall vision of god.

*****

No god can be great on earth in the presence of the poor.

*****

The true purpose of spiritual leadership is to teach man to lead, not to follow. For no man has been born to die another man's death, so too he cannot live another man's life. And each person, to a greater or lesser degree, by virtue of his own goodness, has that talent of the gods to become a god.

This being true, it follows that no one, more than one's self, is responsible for the well-being of the soul. And that this responsibility is carried by the individual day by day, hour by hour, moment by moment.

*****

Everything, would be different, as we've imagined it would be if we stood in the presence of God, because God is free of gravity. We have created god and heaven as an escape from gravity. Gravity is the master of our invention of God; the puppeteer of the dream.

*****

There are differences in man's belief in god but not in the desire to believe.

*****

In the absence of God we would do just as we are now. We would create some means of pitting the good in ourselves against the bad. We would fight for food, family and land. We would be grateful without being naive, hopeful without being blind, and loving without being loved.

*****

God is the most misused, the most misunderstood term in any human language. As advanced as we in the twentieth century appear to be our relationship to God remains primitive.

*****

To be shaped in the image of God, is to be God less.

*****

The difference in levels of intelligence among beings of the fourth dimension is one reason why we have such differences in our concept of god and how man should relate to god.

*****

We could not live with the truth about god.

*****

There is a goodness in man that does not require a god to give it value.

*****

Wars are more frequently started by those who think they are superior than by those who think they are equal or inferior.

Thus a belief in God that permits one to think oneself superior to another must contribute to the creation and justification of war. By this logic God is just vanity; and war in the name of God an expression of vice.

*****

People believe in that God which makes them feel life has a purpose beneficial to them.

*****

Some gods are cannibalistic.

*****

The statements 'I serve God, I love God, God loves me, God directs me,' are abuses of god.

*****

The absence of God does not leave man without hope or an ability to be good to himself and his fellowmen.

*****

To all religions that praise God as the benevolent and just Father of life, I ask, who is responsible for the poor? Who will claim to have created an existence so pathetic and cruel? Who?

*****

GRAVITY

Gravity is an unrefined and primitive force. In being so it is quite in harmony with the unrefined and primitive state of man. The more refined man beecomes the more refined the laws which act upon him.

*****

Once man is free of the womb of gravity, then he will know what god is. A first step we can take is to free our minds from the conditions of gravity by bringing our attention to an awareness of ourselves in the present.

*****

Thoughts were weightless, so when a man becomes to himself a thought his body levitates. To build a gravity repulsion engine requires a knowledge of levitation.

*****

GREATNESS

Cycles of greatness are a result of laws, not men.

*****

No greatness can be achieved without an intentional and directed focus of attention—accident is not a part of greatness. Success based on accident cannot be great success.

*****

H

HABITS

Habits develop when the intervals in a series become too small and the series begins to recur. To break a habit requires opening up the interval for a longer period of time.

*****

To know ourselves by our habits, the repetitive appetites of our likes and dislikes, is not to know ourselves.

*****

HEAVEN

A world without material three-dimensional limits does exist but it is not a tranquil heaven.

*****

The third dimension, when seen from the fourth, is more beautiful, more incredible than we can imagine. All concepts of heaven, based on the idea that heaven is similar to our world of the third dimension come from seeing the third dimension from the fourth.

*****

The comforting belief that failure to acquire peace of mind in this life succeeds in the next one, excuses us from working harder to acquire peace of mind now.

*****

HELL

Hell is that space in man where he creates a need for heaven.

*****

HEROES

God is our greatest hero. He is powerful, never tires, cannot be defeated. He is always right, never wrong, invisible, perfect, wise and He does not exist.

*****

A society that finds heroism in extreme and lunatic behaviour is a society descending toward the second dimension.

*****

I

IDEAS

Ideas, visions, fantasies are responses to emanations entering our bodies. We are generally unaware of the sources of these emanations. And though we cannot logically connect them to 'reality', that does not reduce their influence on our reality. For example, a completely unexpected idea arrives from some distant unknown place; the idea is an emanation which turns into an invention in the hands of a scientist. Idea precedes all invention and invention changes the world.

*****

You can't kill ideas. Ideas are like ants. They live like ants inside the very nature of man. Kill a few and there are many more that will rush out to take their place.

*****

IDENTIFICATION

The greater the degree of identification or attachment that a person has to something the greater the loss of memory and the possibility of having memory.

*****

IDENTITY

Attaching our identity to an already existing series, (to a person, place, or thing—such as a film star, a country, a belief in God) places our identity in the quantas of that series. This is a form of imitation. For true self-expression to come into being, one's identity must be formed within the difficult intervals of one's own life.

*****

We always think I am, I did, I yawned, I walked, I eat, I see, I touched, I talk, I sleep, I love. Were we to examine and dissect what makes a yawn, a laugh, a tear, a call for help, a love possible, it would be difficult for us to say I, because no one I could be responsible for the many parts of so complex a number of processes. Also, saying I too often means that we take simple things for granted, lose that sense of wonder we had as a child before the big, I, became so important.

*****

Note the difference between the awareness of a sensation and the sensation itself. If we give our attention to the awareness of sensation our identity rests with the awareness. If we give it to the sensation it rests with the sensation. Identity in awareness is nearer to the soul. Identity in sensation nearer to the body. The fight over who gets the attention, thus the identity, is the fight between the body and the soul. We get confused when attention is shared by awareness and sensation.

*****

ILLUSION

Illusions are everything to man. Without them the man that we know would crumble. Religion, wealth, freedom, fame, love, all help spread illusion. They keep us believing that we make choices, that the little bit of our brain we use can comprehend the universe and creation, that feelings are eternal, that heaven is free, that we live without conflict after death, that we are alive now. Man cannot live without illusion but he can begin to know he is living with them.

*****

We must ask ourselves: what are we not seeing in what we see; what we are not knowing in what we know; what are we not trusting in what we trust? Where are the illusions?

*****

Substituting one illusion for another is not freedom from illusion.

*****

When illusions are more real and more familiar to us than reality, we do all we can to defend them, to praise them, and to force others to see them too.

*****

An illusion is, quite simply, anything that conceals reality.

*****

IMAGINATION

We spend most of our life imagining where we are rather than being where we are. To be where one is one must refrain from too much imagination about the future or imagining memories of the past.

*****

Observe that imagining oneself to be in the present is effortless, while 'being' in the present requires great effort.

*****

Imagination can be a kind of vision that touches on the fourth dimension.

*****

Goals too difficult to accomplish in reality are often transformed into dreams and imagination. It is possible for dreams to emerge as realities but usually they do not because dreams are comforting and comfort sedates the mind.

*****

IMMUNE SYSTEM

The American Indians and other peoples who understood the harmonies of nature and lived in accordance with those harmonies represented a part of the immune system of the earth. Their purpose was to prevent the spread of diseases that abuse the body of nature. It was not just a sad day for the Indians when the white man took over. It was a sad day for the earth.

*****

IMPRESSIONS

The speed of digestion of impressions by a species or event determines the strength and the quality of memory produced in them: if a species or event is ascending, gaining more possibilities; if descending, losing possibilities. A descending series has less choice, less memory and a slower rate of digestion of impressions than an ascending series.

*****

Impressions are more consistent, more powerful and more diversified than any other food taken in by us. And yet they are not recognized as having any influence.

*****

We are at every moment of our lives, stimulus-response beings. Impressions are there every moment to stimulate us. Were they not there our fragile three-dimensional existence would dissolve immediately.

*****

INFINITY

What we call happiness results from our stepping out of a period of unhappiness. Without unhappiness we would have no need of happiness. Our falling into and out of happiness and unhappiness is based on the interval. We know intuitively that if we could do away with the interval, happiness would be infinite. But in a world of infinities where the duality of up and down does not exist, there is no need for happiness.

*****

Infinities can be achieved by creating constant intervals or by closing intervals completely. In either case the law of seven is eliminated as a deciding force.

*****

INSANITY

Many forms of mental illness result when identity is lost through the breakdown in a person of one of the five laws of body type, alchemy, chief feature, brain centre or essence. For example, an emotionally centred jovial with a gold alchemy, a northern essence and a feature of power is going about her day pushing people around and lecturing on how others should lead their lives. Then one day she falls ill and is deprived of the strength she needs to exercise her power feature. She cannot see herself as someone without control over other people. In the absence of power her identity collapses. Or take a ballet dancer who falls and breaks her leg so badly that she can no longer dance. This would mean the absence of her identity in the Moving brain. The loss of identity in this brain shatters her entire picture of who she thinks she is and what she thinks she can do. People who win vast sums in lotteries face a similar problem if they lose touch too quickly with what they were before they became rich. Any sudden shock that causes a breakdown in one of the five laws can produce mental illness if an adjustment is not made quickly.

*****

INTELLIGENCE

To calculate the level of intelligence of a species we need to realize the ability of that species to survive in the fourth dimension. The tortoise has lived on the earth successfully for millions of years. The length of its lifetime in the third dimension may well be an aid to its survival in the fourth.

*****

No study of the intelligence of man can be comprehensive without knowledge of the five brains.

*****

The higher the level of intelligence the less wasteful the being of that intelligence.

*****

Man's assumption that he is the most intelligent form of life is not the best first step to take in measuring the level of intelligence in other forms of life.

*****

The degree to which a person is aware of himself in the fourth dimension determines the level of that person's intelligence, and his understanding of the creation of wisdom.

*****

Intelligence can be measured by the ability of a species or event to communicate to itself within itself, with other similar and dissimilar types and with the environment in which it lives.

*****

An intelligent being will select from present possibilities those things that will contribute most to a higher degree of greater possibilities.

*****

If complexity results in confusion, meaning is lost and waste increases. With the increase of waste there is a decrease in intelligence.

*****

INTERVAL

Intervals, in what we define as reality, occur when the rate of having perception surpasses the rate of forming definition.

*****

The first interval in human affairs—the weak interval—is characterized by the absence of interest or by slight discomfort or irritation. The second interval—the strong interval—is characterized by exasperation, anger or extreme impatience. On the positive side the first interval can be felt as something mildly positive, pleasant, whereas in the second there would be happiness, joy or love. Another way to detect the interval is to observe that many shocks come in twos—the time or spacing between the two shocks is difficult to determine. You find some money on the way to work, then when you get home that night you are told that you won the lottery. You stub your toe, an hour later you break your arm, an alarm clock goes off, then ten minutes later a siren sounds. The Armenians run from ethnic violence in Azerbaijan only to be buried in an earthquake. The ship's purser on a Philippine ferry survives the sinking of the ferry only to be nabbed and killed ashore. In all cases the second shock in the second interval will be of a similar character, have something in common with the first shock in the first interval.

*****

An example of a multiple-intersecting interval: There is a four-way intersection in downtown New York. Four cars travelling at varying speeds enter the intersection at the same time and crash. One person is unharmed, another has a broken leg, another is almost dead and the fourth has died. Each driver at the approach to the intersection was moving along either the first three or the last four quantas of their respective series. They all met at an interval and left the interval in a completely different direction.

*****

Think of all the things that you decide to do, start to do, but don't complete. So if such things can happen to you can't they also happen to nature, and isn't nature inside something like we are inside nature? And isn't it possible that this thing that nature is in is also subject to intervals? So should we be surprised by oddities in nature any more than we are surprised by an unfinished story, an incomplete thought, an unfinished painting? Intervals happen on so many levels that we can imagine the law of seven as being a kind of blood that flows through the veins of many dimensions as if they were one body. And we might be correct in assuming that the head of this body is god and that we, by being given a home in the little toe of the third dimension are very rarely, if ever, in the mind of this god.

*****

How long can a man live in a state in which he cannot define himself as a man? How long can he live in the interval?

*****

The intervals into and out of our world are frightening because at both these times we are helpless. Fear of death is the fear of helplessness.

*****

Whenever we are faced with the need to make a choice we are in an interval. Knowing about the interval helps us to choose more wisely.

*****

Intervals in the third dimension are often filled by death yet this death of the third dimension is not the same as the death of three-dimensional beings who live within the third dimension. Death of the third dimension takes place when laws of the fourth dimension overpower laws of the third. The complete absence of the presence of gravity and the absolute disappearance of light are effects of three-dimensional death.

In the first stages of a three-dimensional being's death there are still traces of that being's quantas: gravitational weight and the light absorbed by it. When a part of the third dimension dies, no trace is left of what the preceding quantas had been.

All this—the life and death of dimensions, parts of dimensions and beings in dimensions—is a kind of war that goes on between the laws of the second, third and fourth dimensions, a war that is interpreted by us as a battle between good and evil forces.

*****

At death, as with all intervals, there is unpredictability. This makes the future of each intersecting series, while in the interval, quite uncertain. Life after death for man cannot be understood until man is made aware of the influence on his death by multiple intersecting intervals. To assume that everybody goes to heaven or hell at death is incorrect.

At every interval, no matter when or where, there are multiple possibilities. With the increase in dimensions those possibilities increase, but even the lowest-level dimensions have multiple intersecting intervals that are filled by a number of diverse series.

*****

A descending series can be reversed at the intervals and made to ascend just as an ascending series in its intervals can be made to descend.

*****

There are two intervals in a series, yet most of the time we only get as far as the first interval. The degree of importance placed upon a series can determine its outcome. If something is important enough we will pass both intervals. A good place to observe deviations at the first interval is in conversations at parties and social events. There is always some discomfort in meeting new people and in speaking to people we already know who are not interesting to us. So what do we do? We take the first opportunity to change the subject. This first opportunity comes with the first interval. The result is that we are left with a lot of unfinished conversations. Try to remind people you are talking to, to finish their thought, and see what happens.

*****

We generally have less energy at the arrival of the second interval than at the first, and more energy after passing the second. A good example of this can be found in how we resolve problems. In the last interval the difficulties seem too much, yet as soon as we have the answer we feel strong again. The exhilaration seen on the faces of runners after they win a race is a good example.

*****

Whoever or whatever makes the choice at the interval, is god to that interval.

*****

Any spiritual pursuit, even black magic, must appeal to the powers that make it possible to scale the walls of the interval.

*****

If you want to do something new change your job, buy a new car, go to a movie, you can't do it until an interval arrives in what you are already doing. It doesn't matter how hard we try, pray, or wish. No interval can arrive before the completion of the series of quantas that precede it. Once the interval arrives, you can do something. We must realize how important this is. Stopping the law of seven is more difficult than stopping the pull of gravity. A lucky man or a wise man knows how to time himself, to be patient when the possibility for change (in the quantas) is small and to act when the interval comes.

*****

Disastrous events such as the destruction of the Challenger, assassinations, volcanic eruptions and war, when viewed on the scale of the law of seven, are just intervals, necessary interruptions in the course of events that make the third dimension possible.

*****

The shock which forces the passing of the interval can be made of coarse energy, but the species or event which results, in order for it to be an ascending species or event, must produce a finer energy.

*****

A principal element in learning to apply the knowledge of the law of seven is to know that the interval is filled by a shock (a stimulus) and that we, by controlling our attention, can direct this shock.

*****

The points where it is most difficult to build the road, write the song, finish the drive, are the intervals.

*****

'The first fifty dollars are hardest to earn', or 'begun is half done'. These two old sayings refer to the interval that exists before the sounding of the first quanta.

*****

Life in the interval would be like having an idea, an inspiration, a perception, and doing nothing with it, giving it no definition, form or reason for being.

*****

Leaders can arise only in the intervals.

*****

People assume that the interval is bad. For thousands of years this has been the source of man's fear of change.

*****

Without our awareness of the interval there can be no participation on our part in the outcome of the interval. All that we know is that something happened and that we had no choice.

*****

When two people have the same idea at the same time yet are miles apart, we see the fourth dimension entering into the third at two separate intersecting intervals at the same time.

*****

Species and events that are born in and live in the interval are called transitional species and events. They are transitional because they have not passed the interval to acquire the identity of a complete series. They are something born to be what they cannot become.

*****

Most abstract art is a transition between materials and subject matter. What is called a 'finished work' by people such as Pollock, de Kooning, Vedova, Rauschenberg, Burroughs, Johns, etc., goes beyond the bare nature of the materials of the medium, yet not so far as to complete a series. The homosexual is an interval species, he is neither a man nor is he a woman. All incomplete species and events are transitional. Terrorism, riots, mass demonstrations are all transitional events splashing in the interval between war and peace. They are not war and they are not peace. The twentieth century is a transitional century born in the interval between the human earthman and the human spaceman. Religious leaders such as Jerry Falwell and the Bakkers arise in the interval between Powers and Being. They have neither real power nor real being. Mud is a transition between soil and water, dolphins between man and fish, questions between understanding and ignorance. Some giant moths are a transition between birds and insects. Money is a transition between labour and product, etc. etc. etc. . . .

*****

INVENTIONS

The giving to man of such inventions as the boomerang, the wheel, fire, flight, glass, telephones, books, art, etc. is quite simply the giving to us of those foodstuffs which we require from our Carriers in the fourth dimension. They pass these things to us by way of multiple intersecting intervals. And we, like the baby in the womb, know almost nothing of the reasons why that food has been given to us.

*****

J

JUSTICE

Beings within each dimension can actualize possibilities contained within the dimension just above them and the one just below. Thus, any being in any dimension can acquire possibilities of enlightenment or lose them. In relation to gaining or losing possibilities, all beings of all dimensions are equal, and so there is justice. Every angel can fall, every devil rise, a rock, a toad, a wisp of air, space—all can gain or lose possibilities.

*****

And why do we show a greater desire to understand the making of a criminal than to understand the making of a victim?

*****

Justice as we understand it, is that action taken by an individual or group to right a perceived wrong done to an individual or group. A perceived wrong in one situation may not be wrong in another, just as perceived justice in one situation may not be just in another. True justice in the third dimension occurs, when beings of the fourth dimension intervene with the purpose of increasing spiritual possibilities. Those actions undertaken by these beings to this end may appear to us to be unjust, as in the case of the murder of Jesus Christ.

***

JUSTIFICATION

Justification implies that one has rationalized an action so as to permit oneself to repeat that action.

*****

K

KNOWLEDGE

Man does not create knowledge, he receives it.

*****

Knowledge in itself does not give understanding.

*****

Objective knowledge does not require human credibility to legitimize it.

*****

Objective knowledge equalizes men, it does not raise one above the other.

*****

Though objective knowledge is given it must be earned to be understood.

L

LAW OF SEVEN

Passing intervals in the law of seven too quickly can result in assembly-line mentality.

*****

The feeling of being carried along by events that we want to stop or get out of, but cannot stop, is the trap that the law of seven has set for us. Quantas are the bars of the cage.

*****

To verify the law of seven we need only observe and remember what we have seen. The law is here, the choice to verify it or not rests with us.

*****

With the knowledge of the law of seven we can know that we are not able to finish something because we have not passed the final interval of the series. Knowing this helps us to place ourselves into a situation where we can pass the interval.

*****

To see the effect of the past on the present we must know at what point in which series the present is. If the present is at the point of quanta one there is no past. If the present is at the point of completing quanta seven there is no future.

*****

Every series is a series of moments making up one memory. In the first interval, that memory begins to fade. If it fades too much the series ceases to exist, and there is no further memory.

*****

Traffic intersections are good examples of the law of seven and the intersecting interval. If we put ourselves on a street corner waiting to cross the road, the series of cars must stop before we can cross. At the light we see a friend in a car. Because the car is stopped we decide to talk to our friend. His series of driving has reached an interval, our series of waiting has reached an interval, our conversation is an intersecting interval. In the conversation we ask to ride to the next street. He says sure but the door won't open. Then the light turns green, there is confusion, uncertainty about what to do. An unknown has become the active force. This unknown is where the fourth dimension can begin to enter, but we are not accustomed to living with so many possible choices in one moment. We start to get angry, this is too long a period without definition, we want to make a choice right away. We must decide, must get out of this traffic with everybody honking. The door is still stuck, we say forget it, and go back to the curb. A decision has been made, the next quanta has been sounded, the confusion and pressure have passed. Possibilities have been reduced to one action, life is again normal.

*****

Further Examples of the law of seven:

You're walking down the street (Q1-Q2-Q3). Then you stop at a corner as a car goes by (interval). Once the car passes you begin to walk again (Q4-Q5-Q6-Q7). Then you stop again realizing that you forgot something (interval) so you turn around and walk back in the direction from which you started (Q1-Q2-Q3). Then a boy stops you and asks you to help him get his paper plane down from the tree (interval)...

You're mixing the ingredients for a cake (Q1-Q2-Q3), then your cat jumps onto the counter and knocks an open shaker of salt into the pot (interval), after carefully removing the salt you begin again (Q4-Q5-Q6-Q7), then the phone rings (interval), you answer the phone, talk for a couple of minutes then return to mixing the batter (Q1-Q2-Q3) ...

You feel lonely, you're sitting in a chair looking at a blank television (Q1-Q2-Q3). Suddenly you realize you're hungry (interval), so you get up and walk to the store (Q4-Q5-Q6-Q7); at the store you meet a friend (interval), and decide to go to a movie (Q1-Q2-Q3). The movie house is closed (interval), so you say goodbye to your friend and return home (Q4-Q5-Q6-Q7) . . .

*****

The law of seven is a prison in the same way that gravity is a prison.

*****

LAWS

The laws of metaphysics are not diminished by distance or time.

*****

Who can see gravity, hear light, taste magnetism? Who can see, hear or taste the laws of metaphysics? Does gravity exist? Does light exist?

*****

Though the law of three generally manifests itself in the interval of the law of seven, its power is such that it can enter any of the quantas either singly or collectively, and it can utterly consume an entire series or series of series. The law of three in being a higher law than the law of seven, is more powerful than the law of seven.

*****

The law of three manifests more frequently in the fourth dimension than it does in the third.

*****

There are rules to the game of life and death, laws that govern action. Knowing the rules does not mean that we will win, but it does mean that we can know why we win or lose.

*****

Some great need within the law of three forces it to express itself as a complete law.

*****

A third force: that force which acts upon the interval to bring change, is a manifestation of the separate, collective or combined energies of the three forces of the law of three.

*****

Any species or event that completes a series of ascending quantas must, by the measure of that success, generate a number of descending quantas. This makes it clear why many of those following Christ are in fact moving away from him. To the degree that he or any other spirit ascends, there exists behind them the residue of that progress.

*****

The laws of metaphysics prevent four-dimensional beings from existing as four-dimensional beings in the third-dimension, just as they prevent three-dimensional beings from existing as three-dimensional beings in the fourth dimension.

*****

The creation of laws is greater than the creation of worlds, as laws create worlds.

*****

The law of seven is indifferent. This indifference to the individual is characteristic of all laws. Gravity does not care if it pulls on you or if it pulls on me.

*****

Duality results when two of the three forces within the law of three—positive/negative/neutral—are in conflict, and the third is not allowed to enter. An influence from within the body of the law of three must intervene, not on behalf of the two conflicting forces but on behalf of the omitted third force whose influence upon the behaviour of the law has been reduced by the expending of energy in the conflict between the two opposing forces. It is, however, the conflicting interactions between these three forces within the limits of the law of three that provide the fuel for the expression of the law of three. Duality can be understood quite simply as the omission of the third force in the law of three; as something unresolved. Intervals in the law of seven are the breeding ground for dualities. The length of an interval is that period of time spent while waiting for the third force to complete the fusion of the three forces in the law of three, and for that completed force to act as a deciding factor—to shock—the elements in the interval into action. For species and events to be created in the third dimension, all three forces in the law of three must be present in the act of providing a shock to fill the interval in the law of seven. The filled interval then results in a completed series which we experience here in the third dimension as life.

*****

Duality is a bastardization of the law of three.

*****

LEARNING

Learning is not a question of having answers, but one of having questions.

*****

People who say they have the answer do not want to be questioned.

*****

Real learning cannot be predicted. With real learning we are led into a room blindfolded without knowing what we will see when the light goes on.

*****

Dont't apologise for learning.

*****

LIE

Lies benefit from the truth.

*****

Spiritual favouritism is a lie.

*****

Not knowing the truth is not the knowing of lies.

*****

Lies are a weak man's truth.

*****

Some people reveal more of what they really are when they lie than when they tell the truth. Such people tell the most convincing lies.

*****

The facts of life exist apart from and beyond the scope of science and religion. For scientists and religious leaders to claim that they and only they have the keys to the facts of life is a suffocating and cruel lie. Indeed, with life and eternity being so vast it is an utter impossibility that the facts of life and eternity can be reduced to the supposed intelligence of science and religion.

*****

LIVES

A human being has a physical, three-dimensional body and a non-physical, four-dimensional body. The four-dimensional body is a time body, a being which contains at any moment an awareness of all the life of the three-dimensional body. A complete four-dimensional body is born by a Carrier in and of the fourth dimension. The Carrier is god to the infant soul within it which derives its nourishment from the life force of nine unified human lives. Future memory can come from any of the nine lives of the soul. This accounts for the feeling that some people have of having lived in another time and place (reincarnation).

*****

A ninth life human being may not be a saint but he will contain a saint.

*****

Those people who are in the later lives of the soul are those who question, doubt, probe genius, demand much of themselves, and know that there is not much time allotted for the work that must be done.

*****

The nine lives of man, in existing simultaneously in the fourth dimension, are spread out through and within many universes. This implies that more than one earth is in existence at the same time, more than one human race.

*****

A benevolent Carrier creates greater possibilities. A malevolent Carrier reduces possibilities.

*****

The nine lives of the soul can be viewed in relation to the seven-quanta two-interval series of the law of seven. The first difficulty of the soul is its conception in this world of its first lifetime, the first quanta. After sounding the beginning of the first quanta, the ensuing Q2-Q3 quantas— lifetimes—are going to follow the path given to them by the law of seven. All three of the first lives will be more or less regular lives—lives without exceptional hardship or joy. In the later part of the lifetime of the third quanta there begins to be a change in this pattern as the pressure of the interval begins to exert itself. As the third lifetime ends and the budding soul enters its first interval, the life of the fourth lifetime begins to take shape. The fourth lifetime—the first interval life time—is often filled with conflict, unresolved questions, great joy, anticipation and uncertainty. The success of the fourth lifetime often requires the attention of the Carrier and luck. Many people who are struck with a sudden belief in God or who feel that a deep faith in God is necessary for their well-being, are people in their fourth lifetime. With the sounding of the fourth quanta the fifth lifetime begins; this lifetime is often more tranquil. The fifth life is the first survivor of the first interval. The success of this survival is felt as confidence. The lives of the next two quantas, the sixth and seventh lives, are lives in which greater questions begin to arise yet remain unanswered until the sounding of the seventh quanta—the eighth life. Those in the eighth life are in some way certain of man's divinity and are very much aware of how difficult it is to realize this divinity. It is not until the trauma of the second interval is overcome, the completion of the ninth lifetime, that a soul is born. The ninth lifetime is the most difficult of all lifetimes, as it is the point of the greatest possibility of success and the greatest possibility of failure. Failure of the ninth life to achieve the birth of a soul would mean a return of that soul to an inactive suspension of possibilities or a descent into realms of fewer possibilities. The fourth and ninth lifetimes are those lifetimes with the greatest risk as they are the interval lifetimes. In the interval lifetime anything can happen because the certainty of the quantas is not there. This means that in the fourth lifetime a soul can be placed into inactive suspension just as it can in the ninth. With the fourth lifetime there is less to lose. This state of inactive suspension is called purgatory by the Roman Catholics.

One thing we can do to help this soul is to remember that the soul is greater than any single lifetime which has contributed to its growth and birth. Remembering this helps us to take ourselves less personally. The world was not created for what we are, it was created for what we can become.

*****

There is a metaphysical or four-dimensional side to all things on earth, the earth itself, the universe and all time and space. Beings who have walked, swam, or have flown upon the earth have all done so in relation to the earth's evolution and the earth's relationship to the evolution of time and space. At one time the earth needed dinosaurs; for the present, it benefits the planet for us humans to be walking around.

*****

Carriers have no such thing as gender. They are a little like space, giving birth to more, or less space.

*****

A three-dimensional being who represents the ninth life of the soul will experience more future memory and have longer, and more profound perceptions about the nature of man from diverse ages than one from an earlier life.

*****

Life-after-death experiences are entries into the fourth dimension from the third. Generally, this is impossible without the help of a Carrier.

*****

LOVE

Love of evil—love of virtue—they are the same love.

*****

To love does not imply to understand. Yet lovers often feel that they understand each other and that that is why they love.

*****

Love is the positive side of power.

*****

Love is dangerous because while in love we are most trusting.

*****

Love is big, dependence small. When we depend on love, love is made small.

*****

Those who preach fear of damnation cannot speak of love, as love has never been, nor will it ever be, born out of fear.

*****

Love is spontaneous, without order and indisciplined; thus when we fall in love we easily make a fool of ourselves. And the obvious foolishness of the one in love is often repulsive to the one being loved unless the one being loved is equally in love and therefore equally foolish.

*****

Fear of damnation cannot inspire love.

*****

Love is a lie when held at a distance. Only that love is true which can survive hand-to-hand combat.

*****

Love must be proven more than given or received.

*****

M

MAN

Man, who is a being of imagined futures and remembered pasts—an imaginary being—must develop into a Being of the present—a human being—before he can become an enlightened being of the fourth dimension.

*****

Human life is only one possible application of that energy that makes human life possible—just as a nuclear bomb is only one possible application of nuclear fusion.

*****

The constant narration and chatter that goes on inside our head is better understood after verifying the multiplicity of man. Body types, alchemy, features, the five brains, essence etc. all receive and respond to stimulus. And the little theatre in our head plays out the responses to the stimulus while we sit and watch with an occasional laugh or frown.

*****

Man thinks he is special and he may be, but not when he thinks himself so.

*****

Man does not have a soul, it is the soul that has man.

*****

Man, by virtue of his having five brains, a body type, feature, alchemy and essence, has more choices. Therefore, he may be able to achieve a higher level of evolution than the rest of his three-dimensional friends.

*****

No man has become good without first seeing how bad he is.

*****

Man is an incomplete being and as such must accept that his knowledge is incomplete.

*****

It is disconcerting to note how many people are horrified by the prospect of man remaking himself and other three-dimensional creations via the science of genetic engineering. They say genetic engineering is an affront to God, that it dehumanizes man, that the boundaries of propriety are being over-stepped. And those same people are not horrified by the fact that nearly all interpretations of God close the mind and lead to some form of base judgement, discrimination and murder.

Seeing man as a machine, a machine that has parts to adjust and fittings to change just like any other machine is not a bad step to take.

If genetic engineering can help to expose the lie in man's belief that he is uniquely qualified to measure God, I say fine, let's see more genetics, let's see if man can become a creator of life, if he too can make man.

Today man cannot create life yet his belief in a God who can permits him to take life, to kill in the name of God. But man will never fully understand or appreciate life until he can create it as easily as he can destroy it.

*****

Certainly, we know that man is a stimulus-response creation. But do we know what this means?

*****

As was mentioned earlier, man is not as simple as that one-brained ape-like being that crawled about the surface of the earth for the first time millions of years ago. Instead, he is a complex five-brained being of immense possibilities and functions which can be calculated precisely.

*****

We simply cannot go on asking so much about the universe and its creation while knowing so little about ourselves.

*****

The greater the physical strength of the body the more difficult it is to pass beyond physical realities.

*****

To increase the present speed of the cellular human body to that of the speed of light would bring the less important part of man—his material body— into contact with the most important part of man—his spiritual body.

*****

Man is like a work horse, a slave to the fourth dimension.

*****

The hidden side or the inside of man is no less visible than the outside. In other words, his insides are all around him.

*****

It is in the world and not in the home that a man becomes a man.

*****

The admiration that a lesser man has for a greater man, when it touches the greater as idolization, becomes an attempt by the lesser man to pull the greater one down to his level. It is wise to respect those whom we admire through self respect.

*****

Man is such a complex mixture of diverse systems and processes that it would be more accurate, when referring to man, to use the term human systems rather than human beings.

*****

The internal world of man, the world of his dreaming, his imagining, the world of his thoughts, is similar to that endless night in which stars make their home. As we look out at the night sky we assume it to be colourless, yet reason tells us that light radiating out from the sun must fill that space and that to see colour in it, all we need is an object set in space which can reflect sunlight. Were our eyes a fine enough instrument, we would see while gazing at the night sky highly abstract waves of colour rather than darkness—as sunlight, when it impacts upon the changing volume of space, produces colours. Inside man the same is true. Colour results when man is more fully aware of his dreaming. The less aware he is the more black and white things appear. The degree, brightness and texture of the colour are determined by the dreamer's degree of alertness. The alertness itself is the surface upon which the dreams, thoughts, etc., are registered, just as space is the surface upon which colours are registered.

*****

For the same reason that white blood cells group together to defend the human body so do human beings group together to defend the greater body of mankind. The nature of the group—religious, political, social, etc.—is less important than the organizational function of the group itself.

*****

It is not inhuman to speak about the inhumanity of the soul.

*****

Knowledge about man is infinite, yet man himself is finite.

*****

Our great desire to experience the unknown comes from that fragment of the fourth dimension lodged in man's pineal gland at birth.

*****

With the knowledge of body types, brain center, features, alchemy, and essence we can know that we have been given, what we were born with. Chief feature and essence are held over from past lives, they are our karma, but they can still be called given.

*****

Body types account for tendencies not specific actions.

*****

Because body types are influenced by the planets at conception we can assume that we are, to some degree, from the planet or planets which were most influential at our conception. The earth man image that we have of ourselves is not wholly accurate.

*****

The greater a person's attention to detail, the more refined the alchemy.

*****

Copper and lead alchemy are unreliably functional, and lead is more so.

MATHEMATICS

It is a mistake to assume that mathematics is the last word, the ultimate arbiter, in proving the truth of insight.

*****

MATTER

Scientists must accept that emanations are a form of matter and/or anti-matter. The best instrument for measuring the velocity and character of this form of matter is the human being. The human being is an underrated tool with an overrated intelligence.

*****

MECHANICS

The Mechanics of God, is in a sense, a philosophy of the present, as it deals with an examination of the realities that you are experiencing right now wherever you are, doing whatever you are doing.

*****

I have not said to stop what you are doing, to stop what you are believing, feeling or thinking, to change your job. I have said to add to whatever you are doing a greater awareness of your self doing it.

*****

The Mechanics of God is a roughly sketched blueprint for the making of souls.

*****

Laws and processes are the mechanics of god.

*****

All knowledge in *The Mechanics of God* has various levels of application.

As I understand it, the highest level of application comes when an effort to observe leads to the discovery of one's attention and a subsequent directing of that attention to an awareness of oneself in the present.

*****

MEDICINE

No understanding of diet and medicine can be complete without an understanding of the speeds of digestion of the five brains.

*****

MEDIOCRITY

No one would say that they want mediocrity, yet mediocrity is the rule. This is so because creative inspiration cannot take place in the quantas. Since most of our lives are lived in the first three quantas and since we rarely get past the first interval, mediocrity is the norm. One wonders where are all the great men and women of our day? With so many people on the planet should not there be a hundred Rembrandts, a hundred Miltons, a hundred Bachs?

*****

Mediocrity is less giving.

*****

MEMORY

Each of the five brains has a memory which is common to its function, thus emotional events are best remembered by the Emotional brain, moving events by the Moving brain, instinctive by the Instinctive brain, intellectual by the Intellectual brain. The Unifier, in influencing all brains equally, has memory in all brains, including itself.

*****

Impressions, emanations, food, all have a degree of impact on us when they enter our bodies, and digestion is the process of absorbing and distributing that impact throughout the body. Memory is greater when the impact is greater.

*****

Old memories appear more like dreams than memories.

*****

One sure characteristic that defines man is—forgetting.

He forgets what he says minutes after he speaks, what he hears minutes after he hears, thinks minutes after he thinks. He even forgets what he thinks while he thinks it. He forgets what he sees, what he was doing, what he wants to do. He forgets to remember, he forgets everything, he even forgets himself. Between his foregetting and his sleep man lives a little.

*****

In a manner similar to that of the Instinctive brain's use of blood vessels to transport blood, all brains transport their various forms of food throughout the entire human system by way of their related interconnecting parts in each brain as seen in diagram 3. Each part in each brain stores memory according to its function. So a 'three of diamonds' experience, like reading the newspaper will be stored in the jack of diamonds, whereas a loving embrace is remembered by the five of hearts.

*****

Attempting to remember that every moment contains multiple truths, helps us to have multiple thinking patterns and a more diversified memory.

*****

A strong traumatic shock in the future, through the vine of future memory, ripples down into the present as fear of the future. Some seers, in perceiving the nature of this fear, can see the cause of it and tell you about something that you most likely can do nothing about.

*****

The time body of a species or event, is like that species or event's memory of itself. Thus all things, even water, when taken on the level of the fourth dimension, have memory.

*****

Each human being, in being centred in one or another of the brains, by virtue of the energy being focused in that brain, has greater memory of subjects related to it. Intellectually centred people are good at remembering numbers, data, words, etc. Emotionally centred people remember impressions. Moving centred people remember how to do things, and instinctively centred people remember sensory things such as smell or taste, etc.

*****

The development of present memory, that is the ability to remember to keep one's attention in the present,leads to more frequent future memory.

*****

The greater the impact in and on the third dimension by a species or an event, the greater the possibility that that species or event will generate future memory. Memory of the future must always take place in the past. The past and future are conditions of the third dimension. The present is a condition of the fourth. Three-dimensional beings are those beings who live in the past or the future or in the past and future combined. That man imagined he could fly long before the first airplane was built, was not vision or imagination, but a memory. Seeing the future means that man wakes up a bit and remembers what happened to him yesterday when he fell off his bike and got knocked on the head.

*****

The greater the degree of impact the greater the degree of memory. Put quite simply, if you hit a man with a rock he remembers it for a longer period of time than if you hit him with a pebble.

*****

The pineal gland reproduces the capacity for memory of the soul in

the same way that bone marrow reproduces blood cells. The less active
the pineal gland, the fewer the memories, and the more shocking events
need to be for us to have any memory at all. There can be no soul without
memory of the soul.

*****

Memory would be greater if our awareness of attention could remain for
longer periods of time in multiple-intersecting intervals.

*****

Memory decay is different from forgetting. When we forget something
it is still there, but for some reason it has become, at least temporarily,
inaccessible to us. When memory decays it ceases to exist and cannot
be recalled. Memories subject to decay are those which become locked
in the interval. Memory within the quantas is simply buried. Amnesia
or any extreme form of forgetting means that the memory and the holder
of the memory are in an interval. This is why intervals are dangerous.
Much of our sense of 'I' is based on what we remember 'I' to be. In
the interval 'I' does not have the foundation of memory on which to stand.

*****

The following is an example of future memory. A man in New Delhi
was describing to me the sad event of his wife's death. His feelings and
thoughts the day before her death were ominous. With an understanding
that the fourth-dimensional body of that man contains his entire life, and
that the shock of the death of his wife, within the body of that time, is
a major player in the landscape of his memory, we can see that his hearing
about her death was preceded by his memory of the sadness that he would
soon be experiencing. It is often true that no future event of great
importance comes upon us unexpectedly. Were we able to maintain an
awareness of the intelligence of our fourth-dimensional body while in
the third dimension, no future event would be a surprise to us.

*****

Our preoccupation with people from outer space is quite justified when
we realize that future man will be a man from space. This interest that
we have in beings from outer space is a part of future memory.

*****

The reality of a species or event will be impressed upon us absolutely only when that species or event has succeeded in passing both intervals and sounded all the quantas in the series of its creation. When an event is interrupted at the Q3-Q4 interval, the memory of the first three quantas is likely to decay in that interval. When an event is interrupted at the Q7-Q1 interval the memory is still subject to decay, but that decay can be reversed because of the accumulated strength of the quantas. The strongest memory comes from and is contained within those species and events that successfully pass both the intervals and sound all the quantas. When all the quantas are sounded, identity is secure and memory is strong.

*****

Somewhere buried in the body of the human race is the memory of its birth. The memory, were it to be revealed to us, would be too shocking for us to absorb. Who remembers the shock of being born, of seeing light and perspective, of hearing sound for the first time?

*****

For man to remember the birth of a species or event without the distortion of definition, he must experience the interval and shock where the creation of that species or event took place.

*****

Memory in the fourth dimension has a kind of gravitational pull on memory in the third dimension. This attraction helps to expand the connection between the third and fourth dimensions.

*****

All five brains of man have attention. Memory within these brains is based on the duration of the focus of attention.

*****

Memory holds form together.

*****

If we consider how much memory is possible for one human being, just one, in one hour of his walking down the streets of a city. We realize that most of what we remember we cannot recall at will yet it seems certain that the memory is still there. So to whom do our memories belong if they do not belong to us? Memory is like money in the bank, it belongs to us when we know where it is and how to withdraw it. And imagine how much memory there is just sitting there in all the people in the world. Is all that memory, that energy crop, of value to somebody or thing? Is there someone out there making withdrawals from our giant human memory bank?

*****

METAPHYSICS

Metaphysics is not a theory. To say, as many scientists do, that the world of the unseen has no proof of action because it is unseen, is utter foolishness. That would be like saying that the whole of the ocean, which cannot possibly be seen by fish, has no effect on fish.

*****

Many religious leaders claim to possess a knowledge of metaphysics. Most do not possess such knowledge. And scientists claim that metaphysics cannot be verified. Metaphysics stands between science and religion. To verify metaphysics is to prove that there is a science of religion.

*****

The single greatest division between metaphysics and physics is that in metaphysics man himself is used as a tool, whereas in physics man is, for the most part, disregarded. Yet certainly, any attempt to realize the nature of man and the world in which he lives without a deep and serious study of man, is bound to fall short of the goal.

*****

Metaphysics refers to that unseen world through which we pass each moment to live in the world that we see.

*****

MIRACLES

Miracles, and the having of mystical experiences, are the result of the influence of the laws of the fourth dimension overlapping into the third dimension, or the entry of a four-dimensional being into this world. No four-dimensional being can enter the third dimension without being accompanied by the laws of the fourth dimension.

*****

The supposedly inexplicable nature of miracles is a luxury of primitive reason. Twentyfirst-century man cannot afford this luxury.

*****

It is wiser to appreciate miracles than to be surprised or shocked by them.

*****

MOON

With each new and full moon (especially the full moon), man's psyche and behaviour are pushed to extremes, to mostly negative extremes. Little things become big irritations, mistakes mammoth evil deeds. We feel pressure, things will not work out, everything seems too much—too much noise, too much to do, too much traffic, too many people, too much silence. Or we feel great, everything is wonderful, too great and too wonderful. Just observe, and remember how you and others around you, feel, think, and act, two days before, during, and two days after the full moon. After six months of observation you will verify that this is so. And if this is so, what of the other forces, the laws, the other powers bearing down upon our fragile world?

*****

That the moon pulls on the seas to create tides is understood. From this we can deduce that man, in having over 50 per cent of his body made of water, must also be pulled upon. And the pulling must affect his behaviour.

*****

We can observe and know that the full moon affects us physically and psychologically. The psychological effects are the result of the moon's depth of being; that is how alive it is.

*****

The new and full moons stimulate the emotional parts of centres:the queens of centres, which evoke extreme behavior.

*****

MORALITY

Concepts of good and evil which develop into moral code, cannot be regarded as opposites. Instead, they must be thought of as the same force with multiple manifestations. Throughout history, from time to time, country to country, the morals of the people change. What is holy to one is irreverent to another. There is no right and wrong, just differences in the expression of impersonal laws. One second in the fourth dimension makes this clear.

*****

The morality of the soul cannot be defined on the level of human being. This is understandable yet difficult to accept as it puts our morality into question.

*****

MOTION

The mathematics of motion are abstract.

*****

N

NEGATIVITY

Negativity—when it is not controlled and transformed—controls. An awareness of one's attention becomes impossible in the presence of rampant anger, bitterness, hatred, criticism, and judgment. Most of us are unable to control such negativity. But when we realize and accept this limitation, we begin to take the first step toward controlling and transforming it.

*****

Negativity generates heat. Is the sun negative?

*****

In general any form of strong negative emotion or action, though it at first appears to make us strong, eventually weakens us, reduces us just as fire reduces what it consumes. And, though it is rare, there are those who can grow in the fire.

O

OBSERVER

Observation of an event can make it happen.

*****

Observation is greater than definition and much more difficult to live with.

*****

A first step toward the development of a non-participating observer is for one to realize—as would a child—observation without material adult responsibilities. Successful forms of meditation aim at freeing the meditator—for a time—from material responsibilities.

*****

The realization of god: that principle which has the power to direct the changing existence of matter, is an aspect of the vision of the observer.

*****

On the subject of attention we have discovered that we can locate our attention and what it is focused on, and that an increase in awareness based on this effort gives us a greater sense of where we are while doing whatever we are doing. An additional step takes us to the non-participating observer of that awareness of our attention. And we must note that the observer is intelligent.

*****

The observer is a category of being in the fourth dimension which, when added to the consciousness of man, creates divine perception—the seeing of things without the aid of light and the human eye.

*****

OCCUPATIONS

The work that we find ourselves doing is directly related to the lifetime that we are in now. With greater awareness man can see what he has done in past lives and understand why he is doing what he is doing today. For example, in the second lifetime a man might be a bricklayer because in the second lifetime it is necessary for the growing four-dimensional foetus to feed on the sweat of the body. In another lifetime there is torture and sorrow, in another riches and power, in yet another moderation and wisdom.

*****

P

PERCEPTION

All new perceptions, new realizations about oneself and the world in which we live, are degrees of penetration into the fourth dimension.

*****

How different our perception of the world would be if everyone had 50-50 or 2-2 vision.

*****

Perception in the fourth dimension takes place in the absence of light, gravity, and all other material laws, while at the same time seeing as those laws see.

*****

An increase in awareness produces an increase in perception, and perception is not merely an expansion of the eye, but an expansion in the receptivity of all the parts of man.

*****

The force of an incoming perception defines that perception, and creates in one the decision as to what the perception was.

*****

From the fourth dimension, objects in the third dimension are seen, in a sense, as from inside themselves.

*****

No man can have greater wealth than perception from the fourth dimension.

*****

Perception is the eye of a fourth-dimensional being.

*****

PERSONAL

Not taking things personally does not mean that one does not feel but that one uses one's feelings as a tool to act rather than to react.

*****

PHENOMENON

The fall of California will not occur so much as a result of the motions under the coast, as from an interval in the usual balance of influence exerted on the earth by the fourth dimension of our solar system's larger planets. That is, the spark that will set off the slide will come from within the body of the fourth dimension of the planets. Jupiter and Saturn are competing in the fourth dimension for the right to express an evolutionary effect on our solar system in the third dimension. The result of this conflict will bring trauma to those species and events of the third dimension. And something completely new will come out of it.

*****

PHYSICS

Physicists, in having moved much closer to the mysteries with their ruthlessly sterile instruments, must be watched closely. Unwrapping the present carelessly can prove disastrous. Laws must be obeyed, not ignored. Do we run to the top of buildings and jump off thinking that we will not hit the ground? No. This would be abuse of gravity. Abuse of the greater laws of metaphysics could stop our growth as a race, or even discontinue the race.

*****

It is surprising how big and bulky is the machinery that we are using to extend our knowledge and observation of matter into the fourth dimension; and how simple it is for emanations from the fourth dimension to enter the third.

*****

PINEAL GLAND

The pineal gland is that natural aspect in man which interfaces with the fourth dimension.

*****

The pineal gland is the stomach of the soul.

*****

POLITICS

The male's predominance in politics is not necessarily bad, but his ability to govern would be much improved by the reduction of his disrespect for the emotional perceptions of women.

*****

Countries like Russia need not fear losing the majority of their people if they opened the door because the law of seven would not allow it. For that to happen a large number of people would need to be experiencing the same interval at the same time. This can happen, as it does with a revolution, but in general does not.

*****

POLLUTION

We must be concerned about pollution, as man, when seen on the scale of the earth's fourth dimension, behaves much like a cancer; and the earth, much like our bodies, will do all it can to remove this cancer.

*****

POWER

The power concentrated in a multiple-intersecting interval is beyond our means of imagination, its effect being that much greater than any human invention or comprehension of power. Any thing, person, or creature that can control the dynamics of the interval has at its disposal the power to create or destroy any and all manifestations of the law of seven. Enlightened beings such as Buddha, Shakespeare, Christ, Socrates, etc., are examples of men who had a degree of this power. Man, as a species, in the distant future will have, as a normal consequence of his changing being, those powers which we now ascribe to God.

*****

PRAYER

Prayer is an effort, not a request.

*****

An effort made to focus attention on oneself in the present is true prayer.

*****

Man often prays because he cannot face the assumption of responsibility for his mistakes.

*****

Praying to relieve oneself of guilt justifies guilt. Mistakes are made for learning, guilt robs us of learning.

*****

PREMONITION

When an event which has happened is strong enough to form a deep impression on our four-dimensional body, that experience comes to us here in the third dimension as a premonition. Premonition is future memory. That is, not a mystical experience, not something to take great pride in or something which sets one apart from the rest of the human race. All people are subject to and capable of having future memory.

*****

Premonitions of a negative nature can be related to the descent of a four-dimensional species or event, or to an illegitimate entry of the fourth dimension into the third.

*****

PRESENT SPEED

Present speed (the speed at which emanations come into and pass out of the present) is increased in relation to the individual who has less of his identity attached to the subject upon which attention is focused. Emanations arriving at present speeds much faster than the speed of light exist all the time. Placing our identity in the awareness of attention, increases our ability to digest greater present speeds. The process of digestion of greater present speed allows us to gain the strength needed to enter the fourth dimension. Greater present speed refers to how deeply a feeling is felt, how long a memory lasts, how fast an emanation travels from its source of origin to the receiver ... In general greater present speed means more of everything: more hearing in what we hear, more seeing in what we see, more understanding in what we understand, more feeling in what we feel.

*****

Light enters into and passes out of the present at 186,000 miles per second, when present speed is one second. Present speed can be one day, one hour, one minute, one second, one millionth of a second, etc. What we call emanations are energy sources that travel at all possible times of present speed. Thus, there are many emanations that travel faster than the speed of light.

The speed of light, as it is measured by the best of man's scientific tools, is the fastest known speed of a materially visible particle that passes into and out of the present.

*****

There are multiple present speeds in the same present moment.

*****

PROCESSES

Ideas as a process are the descent of perception into form, form into habit, habit into tradition, tradition into crystallization. At the stage of crystallization, identification (what Eastern philosophies call attachment) enters. Identification is the cause of unchangeability in man. An identified man cannot hear new ideas, think new thoughts, accept diverse truths, feel other feelings. He is a man trapped in a non-visionary cell with little or no possibility of becoming different. When a perception has decayed to this level it has passed from the fourth dimension into and through the third, and into the highest level of the second. This process of degeneration is a possibility with the arrival of any new idea. To protect ourselves from this downward curve, we must use an idea to generate new perception, thinking and contemplation.

*****

All men, for the good health of their souls, must contemplate, yet few do.

*****

The process of one series developing into a recurring series is the process of creation.

*****

Everything that we experience as life on earth comes to us by way of processes. The law of seven has a major influence on the creation and development of those processes.

*****

Once a species or event has been activated its development proceeds by way of genetic inheritance and/or a combination of morphic resonance and gene selection. According to the law of seven these moments of development are represented by the quantas of a series. The influence of a higher power on a given species or event is unnecessary unless there is a need to alter the entire process in the intervals. Therefore, we can surmise that all habitually repeating events, such as most of human life, exist without direct intervention on the part of higher powers, just as a printing machine once started, need not be stopped unless a change is required.

*****

The qualities of a material determine what influences can affect that material within the intervals of that material's existence. For example— the holes in the ozone layer are intervals in the ozone which must be filled by some force that is compatible with that ozone. An interval in one's thinking would not be filled by that which is used to fill an interval in granite stone.

*****

PROPHECY

Predictions of the future which relate to the quantas of a series or to the series as a whole, are not unusual. For example, prophesying that the coast of California will have a major quake by 1998 would be a good guess, not a prophecy. To predict that a boy in Afghanistan will discover an ancient tool used by the citizens of Atlantis would be real prophecy because there is no associated relationship between the event of the prophesy and present circumstances. True prophetic vision takes place in the multiple intersecting interval, and is unrelated to the quantas of existing species and events.

*****

R

REALIZATION

Realization is a form of intelligence that recognizes the direction in which things must go to sound the first quanta after either the Q3-Q4 interval or Q7-Q1 interval.

*****

REALITY

What is and is not real is relative to which dimension one is in. Certainly, that which has substance and importance in the third dimension has little or no substance in the fourth. So, from the point of view of a being of the fourth dimension, the third dimension and all three-dimensional values are irrelevant.

*****

Reality is measured by the increase or decrease of possibilities. A greater reality contains greater possibilities.

*****

REINCARNATION

Recurrence is greater than reincarnation.

*****

Migration is a part of recurrence.

*****

Reincarnation deals with the reappearance of a soul in different bodies. Where recurrence deals with the same bodies recurring infinitely. And recurrence exists because laws are processes rather than isolated events.

*****

RELIGION

Religion is more a political and sociological force than a spiritual force.

*****

Religious leaders and their groups call that which they cannot convert less good or even evil.

*****

Religion during the time of its conception is, in general, the expression of an ascending series, because at the time of conception it works as a force to open and educate people to the wonders of the fourth dimension. But once established as a definite form, its creative power is forced into the decay of a descending series.

*****

Most religions do not evolve the individual toward enlightenment because they fail to teach the individual that he must be in the present: must know and be true to himself. Instead they teach rejection of the present for the comfort and habit of ritual, ceremony and form.

*****

All forms of fundamentalism kill the soul by institutionalizing the belief that extreme and uniform behaviour is divine.

*****

If man has an ability to learn, to question, to doubt, and if God made man, then God made man to learn, to question and to doubt. Then religious leaders who deny a man learning, questioning and doubt, deny God.

*****

Dictating esoteric doctrine is an illegitimate communication of esoteric doctrine.

*****

Small-minded, small-town religious groups are always more defensive of their leaders, ideas and practices.

*****

Great religion teaches integration of differences rather than division of differences.

*****

Misinterpretation and abuse of religious doctrine is the norm, not the exception.

*****

Most religions isolate, formalize and shrink our relationship to the world rather than to expand and immortalize it.

*****

The fourth dimension is the absence of those illusions which make organized religion possible.

*****

Religion does not change people. Without it, kind people would still be kind and ruthless people, still ruthless.

*****

Religion provides a form, the hope of an often unrealizable ideal, a system of values which people can live with comfortably. Religion is not an enlightening force, as recognizable enlightenment occurs on the level of individuals, not groups. Yet all religious groups claim to be unique and to give to the individual within that group something of God apart from the rest of humanity. This uniqueness may have been true on the level of that group's original leader, yet the religious order which defines and confines its followers in a specific line of thought and behaviour is far from that leader's original contact with the fourth dimension. All great religious leaders had access to the being and intelligence of the fourth dimension beyond a level which could be imagined by their followers. The creation of form is the weaker side of leadership. Form contains people; it does not take them somewhere or change them.

*****

Religions in themselves are neither good nor bad, but people are. A vain man, a powerful man, a greedy or perverted man, when given a religion will use it to express his vanity, his power, his greed or perversion, just as he would use money, social status, friends and loved ones.

Yet when a man uses religion to express his vices, as opposed to the use of money or loved ones, he always says to those who disapprove of his actions, that they disapprove not of him but of the superior religious code that he follows; therefore such disapproval is wrong because they simply cannot see that behind all that he does are the divine truths that he believes in. Once armed with this justification no vice can be contained as it becomes, in the mind of the man who expresses it, an act of God.

*****

Most people feel that they have little spiritual value when they stand alone. So they join a religious group or cult that professes to have contact with God. Once dependence upon that group is secure the individual within the group supposes that he now has God at his side and is that much superior and wiser then all those outside the group.

All religious groups provide this same illusion. And there are very very few religious leaders who will discourage the propagation of this illusion because this is the illusion that buys the leaders cars, houses, clothes, the illusion that provides for sex abuse and the abuse of power.

*****

Religious and scientific debate have more to do with illusion versus illusion, rather than illusion versus reality.

*****

Religion justifies ignorance, fear and prejudice but the worst of these is ignorance.

*****

Religious dictators rape the soul.

*****

The call for unquestioned subservience and obedience to the doctrine and leadership of religious organizations freezes doubt. Without doubt a great religion cannot be made greater nor can it be proven to be great.

*****

S

SANITY

To reduce the possibility of mass insanity leading to mass suicide, man is gradually being prepared for a fourth-dimensional reality. Though abstract art is badly done as an art form, it is helpful, in general, as a tool to free man from the confines of his recognized and habitual reality.

Bigger telescopes, cult groups, genetic engineering, space travel, out-of-body experiences, etc., all help to increase man's tolerance for the unexpected. To embrace the fourth dimension requires great tolerance as nothing for man can be more shocking.

*****

After an unexpected ride through the fourth dimension, the usual difficulties in the life of a man can be magnified, and in some cases compounded negatively by a realization of how empty life has been. The uncertain meaning of the ride can be shocking, even frightening. Also people who have not had a fourth-dimension experience may reject and despise a person who has. Rejection can drive an otherwise normal person really crazy. Usually people either don't realize that they had an altered state or they keep the experience to themselves pretending that nothing ever happened. But many people believe that the shock of an altered state was a good thing, that for a moment everything seemed so magical, so harmonious, and that they felt a great optimistic hope. For these people the sanity of the third dimension is held in balance with the insanity of the fourth.

*****

SCALE

Having a sense of scale implies an ability to perceive the harmony that exists in multiple levels of truth, and is an aspect of man's undeveloped sixth sense. With a sense of scale, man can begin to see the objective importance of a species or event.

*****

Subjectivity is fertilized by the absence of a sense of scale.

*****

SCIENCE

Most scientific reasoning reveals little of the greatest mysteries. And it is surprising that science is so proud of so little. Without this addictive pride science would be truly great.

*****

The mysteries are not exclusive to scientific methods, as life is not exclusive to only one man. No single tool or process created by man can reach farther into the unknown than can man himself.

*****

Science is limited by its belief that discovery is invention. This error causes scientists to view their work as acts of creation.

*****

Waiting to be discovered at the bottom end of the emanation spectrum are several particle-like structures which behave more like an emanation than like a particle of matter. These half-breed realities will come into view with the invention of the Repulsion Engine. The principal function of the repulsion engine will be to transport heavy matter, like people, by way of the generation of anti-gravity force fields which are repulsed by gravity.

*****

Isn't the 'desire to know' the essence of science, and isn't the wonder of discovery and knowing, open to all fields of study?

*****

SCIENTISTS

Because of the exceptional prestige and insights of Stephen Hawkings many people who would normally lack interest in physics have become interested. And Hawkings, whether he wishes it or not, has joined Rupert Sheldrake in bringing society another step closer to a much needed reappraisal of the relationship between physics and meta (beyond) physics. Man's reality is many many times greater than his knowledge and awareness of that reality.

*****

SECOND DIMENSION

The widespread use of television and cinema has introduced several very interesting and challenging considerations.

The screen, no matter how well it depicts three-dimensional life, cannot replace it. It can, when used to its greatest potential, lead the viewer to the doorway of the fourth dimension. As it is now, most viewers unknowingly give the life force of their attention to the screen's two-dimensional world without even considering the long term effect it will have on them personally, or on our race as a whole.

When man's attention leaves him and his three-dimensional world, for the second dimension, he, by way of the lower level of possibilities in the second, reduces his possibilities. So what do we have when a man spends a quarter of his life sitting in front of a TV? We have that much less of a three-dimensional man and that much more of a two-dimensional one.

While watching TV or film we should always remember that we are sitting in a room in a three dimensional world. In the absence of this distinction we assume the heroes of that second dimension to be greater than they are. Then, when we encounter them in the flesh in three dimensions, we are shocked either by the realization that we thought they were much bigger, more dynamic, more beautiful, or we reduce ourselves by superimposing on them that two-dimensional giant which we remember from the screen.

What effect does all this have on the race? One effect is that of reducing the appreciation of three-dimensional life. A leaf, flower or lake becomes less beautiful when compared to a TV screen. How many people take a picture of a place as proof that they were there? The illusion of fame is spread by our acceptance of the second dimension as a three-dimensional reality. What would many a film star, politician and artist be if society had only a personal three-dimensional contact with them? Addiction to newspapers, magazines and TV causes us to abuse the environment because it breeds insensitivity to the environment.

Mountain people, country people, farmers and ranchers, etc., abuse the environment much less than city people who often have a steady two-dimensional diet. One thing to remember about dimensions is that each one has the power to act as a deciding force in the interval. Certainly something happens when we pour our three-dimensional worth into the second.

*****

SELF-RELIGION

A self-religious person is going to find religion in all that he does. He is not going to require the support of a group to identify his beliefs. Neither will he lead nor follow. For him god will not be subjected to definition.

*****

Self-religion provides for the process of learning that religion is not without faults.

*****

A self-religious person is motivated and directed by verification rather than by beliefs.

*****

A person who has spiritual or religious feelings about life and creation yet does not prescribe to a particular religion or faith, is a self-religious person.

*****

For the self-religious, god is often described, quite simply, as the power of creation. There are no strings of religious conduct tied to observing this power nor are there strings tied to respecting it. No material gains are levelled against it and the conversion of other people to this point-ofview is not expected as the self-religious, who have no desire to be converted, have no desire to convert.

*****

Self religion implies a willingness and an ability to observe oneself and to correct one's own faults.

*****

Followers who have been taught to feel religious guilt, believe that all men are born with guilt. Thus any non-religious person who does not feel religious guilt must be made to feel guilt from being non-religious. All the derogatory terms affixed on non-believers by believers, terms like atheist, pagan, philistines, outcaste ... are aimed at intimidating the selfreligious into feeling guilt.

*****

Religious guilt is a psychological parasite attached to the masses by religion—a parasite which succeeds in maiming the very beneficial process of learning from one's mistakes.

*****

To assume that divinity cannot exist outside the formal definitions instituted by the Church, poisons the very essence of man.

*****

The three-dimensional morality of today's man on earth is heavily influenced by man being sucked down to the earth by the earth's gravity. Blood flow is conditioned by gravity, digestion and breathing are conditioned by gravity. Change man's focus of gravity, suspend him in space as the planets and stars are suspended, and you change the blood flow. With a change of blood flow we change a major guideline to our perception of reality. Self-religious man of the future will acquire an awareness of the multi-dimensional reality of the stars and planets when he, like them, is born and bred in the suspended incubation of space.

*****

Doubt is a common characteristic of the self-religious.

*****

Those people who are inspired by the wonder and power of creation without feeling a need to consign that inspiration to the various Gods provided by traditional religion are self-religious people.

*****

Where the religious idolize and worship, the self-religious respect and admire.

*****

A self-religious person does not oppose traditional forms of religion, yet he cannot be a part of them unless they contribute in some way to his basic human needs.

*****

For the self-religious the events of everyday life are religious events. The ritual of life itself is ritual enough.

*****

Man is not born with guilt, he is born with the fear that judgments made against him could cost him his home, family, vocation and possibly his life. A self-religious person is not without fear of judgment but he is not motivated by judgment to feel guilt.

*****

Bulls, falcons, cats, comets—they are the self-religious of nature.

*****

The self-religious prefer the loneliness of religious liberty to the bondage of formalized groups.

*****

Self-religion is the religion of individual freedom.

*****

Self-religion is the oldest and most eternal religion.

*****

SEX

A too rigid sexual morality calcifies thought.

*****

The different attitudes that people have towards sex are generally categorized as moral differences. And the connotation is given that the desire for sex is just a desire and not a need. But how can this be when we recognize that some people have a greater need for books (Intellectually centred people) and others a greater need for exercise (Moving centred people). Instinctively centred people and the martial and mercurial types all have a greater need for sex but this need, when it is expressed within a religiously moral society, is called lust.

*****

The act of having sex is one of our most graphic examples of a multiple-intersecting interval between the beings of the third dimension and possibilities in the fourth dimension.

*****

That moment in which orgasm takes place contains a four-dimensional level of increased possibiliites. Sexually prudent human beings, capable of frequent orgasms in diverse times and places, stand at the apex of higher possibilities for three-dimensional beings.

*****

An orgasm is the expression of Q7 as the last quanta of a series passing the Q7-Q1 interval to the Q1 of a new series. Understanding is an orgasm of the mind resulting from the combined labour of the heart and mind. It is rare for the Q7-Q1 orgasm to be followed by another orgasm right away, as another series of quantas and two intervals must be passed before another orgasm can happen. This can be verified by the study of physical sex. How many people, male or female, can pass from orgasm to orgasm?

*****

Males have predominated over females as an evolutionary force for thousands of years because their command over the moment of orgasm has given them a greater assurance that they can control their destiny. The female's orgasm, in being subjugated to the male's, oppresses the self-satisfaction and confidence that the female needs to assure herself that she too can effect the evolutionary trends in her life. When the female gains control of the orgasm Christ will be a woman.

*****

The male, for the most part, has neglected the female and his own higher possibilities, by assuming that the climax under his control was designed primarily for his pleasure.

*****

The orgasm's greatest power lies in its ability to unify the diverse processes and differences of one being with those of another.

*****

For the body of man to merge with the body of the soul he must yield fully and unconditionally to the soul. Orgasm reveals that unconditional surrender is possible. At the moment of climax nothing is more important than the climax itself and the present moment in which it takes place. All past and future distractions are gone.

*****

When the moment of orgasm is shared simultaneously by both the man and the woman, sex has done all it can do to reveal the existence of the fourth dimension.

*****

Attitudes about sex, which influence the morality of our behaviour throughout our life, begin with the influence on us as children by the attitudes that our parents have which we imitate. Attitudes about sex are the greatest influence that a parent exerts over its child.

*****

Attitudes about sex are always learned and almost always selfish.

*****

The principal motivating force which determines an individual's choice of lifestyle comes from that person's attitude about sex. Thus a person who views sex as necessary only for the bearing of children will choose a lifestyle hat supports the act of having sex only as an act of child-bearing. A perverted person whose attitude about sex includes the seduction and molestation of young boys will arrange his lifestyle in a way that will facilitate seduction.

A casual person with an all-round permissive attitude about sex will be motivated to live a sexually casual lifestyle. Someone who believes in celibacy may choose to be a priest, nun or hermit. In all cases the differences in lifestyle are seen as differences in attitude about sex.

*****

Death is 'Big Sex' as it represents the greatest orgasm of our life. At the moment of death we are made to merge unconditionally, our visible three-dimensional body with that of the invisible four-dimensional body of a developing soul or souls.

*****

It is beneficial for us to prepare for the moment of death by attempting to be in the present now, in this moment. Repeated attempts to focus attention on ourselves in the present build in us the energy needed to release a three-dimensional identity into a four-dimensional one. The view that sex is meant primarily for pleasure and the creation of babies detracts from its greater purpose of revealing to us that talent which we possess to merge harmoniously the properties of two very different worlds.

*****

Men and women should attempt to recognize and share the power of the orgasm. But usually they do not. The rule is that the male overpowers the female; he has his climax, and she does not. The woman is then left to retaliate by whatever means she has available to her.

*****

All species in the third dimension propagate in the intervals of the law of seven. Species such as rocks, which have fewer possibilities, propagate infrequently over very very long periods of time.

*****

The motivation behind all that humans do, think, feel, desire, pray for, love, believe in, die for, trust, hate, fear, expect and pursue is sex and attitudes about sex.

*****

Making love is closer to sex than just having sex.

*****

Sex is a more powerful word than god—more like god than god is like himself.

*****

SHOCK

Traumatic shocks are those moments or periods in which a person, or persons experience a major contradiction in what they understand to be normal life. Contradictions are ignited by the presence of the fourth dimension.

*****

If we are told that this medicine is going to make our injury worse before it gets better, we will not be surprised or frightened when we see that the injury has enlarged and reddened. We won't be unduly shocked because we were told in advance. So too if we are told that such things as future memory, flashes of things to come, ESP, premonitions ... are examples of momentary influences arriving from the fourth dimension. The surprise of the shock should be reduced and a more productive relationship to these phenomenan established.

*****

Unusual species and events shock us because we think they should be different, not because they are shocking. Definition need not precede understanding. This being so, unusual species and events need not shock us.

*****

SIN

'Original sin' is an idea that comes from the creation in the human being of features ('the tragic flaw'). The very basic, dualistic nature of features pits men and women against one another. The mistaken assumption that woman (Eve) is responsible for the failings of man (Adam) is simply untrue, as both men and women partake equally of the debilitating nature of features.

*****

The Instinctive brain's aim to control and manipulate the conscience is sin.

*****

SLEEP

One unfortunate byproduct of sleep is the absence of memory. Were we able to sustain memory, producing experiences twenty-four hours a day, entering the fourth dimension would not be so difficult for us.

*****

SOCIETY

Just as disease is prevalent in the decline of good health in man's body, so is social decay prevalent in the decline of the good health of society. Abuse of religion, carelessness with nature, rampant perversion and molestation of the young, demonstrations, riots, fear and mass hysteria are all symptoms of the decline of social health.

*****

SOUL

The soul is inhuman—it cannot be imagined, and it has needs.

*****

The soul has an appetite; a hunger for the substance of three-dimensional beings.

*****

The amoeba is a perfect three-dimensional being because it has fewer needs to encumber it. Man is the most imperfect of three-dimensional beings. This makes him better suited to feed the soul.

*****

As with the intake of food by the human body, intake of food by the soul is selective. For example, when a man acts deceitfully he threatens to poison the soul particularly if the soul is a young soul on its first or second life. An older soul can take more abusive energy, such as violence, and transform it into perception. Human contemplation is good for the soul throughout all its lifetimes.

*****

We must first learn of the needs of the soul before attempting to live by those actions which best satisfy its needs. We are ignorant of many things, but it is our ignorance of the needs of the soul that produces our greatest mistakes.

*****

The soul is, in essence, a singular harmony of contradictions.

*****

The greatest of great souls as well as the least and most pathetic of souls, leave no traces, no followers, no books, rituals, ceremonies, etc., behind them when they depart from the third dimension.

*****

SPECIES AND EVENTS

The greater the possibilities of change within a species or event the greater the number of influences which can act upon that species or event in the interval where change takes place. The more flexible a thing is within itself, the greater the flexibility of that which can act upon it. The metaphysical and chemical composition of man is our best example of this, as he contains multiple and complex possibilities that can be acted upon by even greater, more complex species or events. Thus, the value of a transition between species and events is measured by its wealth of possibilities. The greater the number of possibilities the greater its value. God, then, being that thing in man's mind which refers to the greatest value, must contain the greatest of possibilities. That moment in which all possibilities of all laws in all dimensions of all times meet, would be god to all other degrees of possibility beneath it.

*****

With eternal recurrence one body is used over and over and over again until the spirit has risen out of it. The times and places of those recurrences could be anywhere and in any time. Recurrence—the process of connecting the interlocking motions of ascending and descending spirals, brings the recurring body to points of transition which allows for that body's recurrence in whatever time and place the spirals meet. All three-dimensional species and events are recurring infinitely in the fourth dimension and spirits of varying levels of being are being processed and born in them. It's a little like the same field having many different crops in different seasons.

*****

We do not know for certain which species or events contain the greatest possibilities of enlightenment. This is why we do not know what we are doing when we destroy a species, kill a dolphin, smash a bug or pollute a lake.

*****

Any species or event that overpopulates is reduced to its most primitive level of existence.

*****

SPACE

Shall we assume that man can live in space armed with only a three-dimensional reality? Or should we take it upon ourselves to reason that he cannot, and that we had better begin to acclimatize to this truth by expanding our sense of reality into the fourth dimension?

*****

There is no being or animal that man will encounter in space that can abuse, mistreat, and torture him more than he abuses, mistreats and tortures himself here on earth.

*****

Space is the spirit of matter.

*****

When man has achieved his intended strength as a being of great time and great space, his appearance and substance will return to that near foetal species that he was while suspended in the womb.

*****

There is visible space and there is invisible space. We see visible space as the distance between visible objects. We see invisible space as that space wherein visibility goes when it passes out of the reach of our senses, such as at death.

STATES

Altered states do not imply an identity in the fourth dimension, though altered states may reveal the existence of the fourth dimension.

*****

The decline of mystical states into human weaknesses is a greater problem than that of creating mystical states.

*****

STIMULUS

Man is an associative stimulus-response being. Type, feature, alchemy, etc., are all given and each represents a difference in how stimuli are processed. There can be no choice of action for an associative stimulus response being. By developing an awareness of oneself in the present we can see what is stimulating us and the effect that the stimulus could have, then choice is possible.

*****

SUICIDE

People kill themselves because they have not been getting enough attention.

*****

Suicide is the most extreme form of vanity.

*****

Any form of suicide or ritualistic murder is invalid as a means of spiritual advancement.

*****

To assume rule over the death of one's own or any other person's body is to assume as well the ability to create a body. Who among the living or the dead can create what he would destroy?

*****

T

TEACHING

He is not a great teacher who burdens his students with the responsibility for his mistakes.

*****

Manipulation for personal gain is not teaching.

*****

We teach how we learn.

*****

We will more often find a student capable of learning than a teacher capable of teaching.

*****

Someone who chooses or is chosen to teach before he has learned, can neither be a teacher nor a student.

*****

More than being concerned with how to teach, a teacher must be concerned with how a student can learn.

*****

To remain a teacher a teacher must continue to learn as a student.

*****

A teacher who lies to teach, deceives.

*****

There are many teachers and many methods for achieving an awareness of ones self in the present. Then look for a non manipulative teacher as the absence of this defect in character is the best measure of a teachers value.

*****

A real teacher will answer questions where a false one will dictate answers. In the first case one can learn, in the second case all one can do is follow.

*****

Teaching can limit learning.

*****

THERAPIST

Most people go to see a therapist, psychologist, or psychiatrist, because they miss the attention—not the love but the attention—of their mothers.

*****

THOUGHT

Thought is an emanation that travels faster than the speed of light.

*****

Any truly new thought comes from the fourth dimension. This can be proven by observing that at the moment of the conception of thought there is an apparent absence of past memory and future imagination.

*****

Man's need to think linearly, logically and in a well-ordered manner is due partly to the effect on his psyche of his physical need to balance himself as he walks, sits, rides a bike, etc.

TIME

The history of time is the time body of time.

*****

When we have the unusual sensations of no time at all or time forever, the sense that everything is happening in slow motion, that what is happening is happening to someone else, the feeling that you have been here before—these are moments of transition into the fourth dimension. Were we able to evoke at will and prolong these moments, we would possess the qualities and being of a saint.

*****

A fundamental difference between time and velocity is that time in the present cannot produce change, and velocity can.

*****

Time, at the point of entry into the fourth dimension, ceases to exist.

*****

Timeless laws cannot exist without time.

*****

Time is a great invisible body without material substance or form which we believe has a powerful effect on our lives. Then why don't we worship 'time'?

*****

TIMING

Timing is that often illusive creature which tells us when to or not to do something. Observation of the law of seven helps give us a better sense of timing. For example, today a friend and I were having coffee together with two ladies. Next to us, in a small alley two boys began to fight. For the first three quantas Q1-Q2-Q3 we just sat there wondering what to do. Fortunately, at just the right moment (Q3-Q4 interval) my friend jumped up to stop them from bashing each other. His good timing was due to the fact that the interval had arrived. Had he or I made an attempt to stop the fight in the quantas we would have run the risk of getting into the fight ourselves. The only right time to attempt change is in the interval.

*****

Timing cannot be taught so much as it can be learned.

*****

TRANSITION

A transitional species or event can become a fixed form if the ensuing direction of that species or event passes the first interval of its conception and completes both intervals of the series.

*****

189

Transition is concerned with what gives rise to species and events, not with what species and events turn into once they are created.

*****

For any three-dimensional being to begin the process of transition from the third to the fourth dimension he must challenge his regard for heaven and hell. It is very difficult for man to identify himself as man without heaven and hell. Yet for him to merge the body with the soul, he must.

*****

TRANSMITTERS

All forms, animals, plants, people, fish, birds, snakes, are different qualities of energy (just as the five brains and their parts represent different qualities of energy). We do not know which of these is the best conductor of transmissions between the third and fourth dimensions. It may be that we are unknowingly cutting ourselves off from certain levels in the fourth dimension by the endangering of species.

*****

TRUTH

Truth and lie both survive the test of time.

*****

Truth has no religion.

*****

We have faith because we believe in illusions. Were the truth known faith would be destroyed, as truth has no need of faith.

*****

Truth cannot be loved.

*****

It is greater to learn the truth than to teach it.

*****

The best way to pursue truth is through what you can verify on a moment to moment basis. Theory without verification leads to belief in theory as the truth.

*****

A person who seeks the truth must also tell the truth.

*****

Faith allows man to believe that he is free to choose what is or is not God. Truth eliminates freedom of choice. This is why most people choose faith over truth.

*****

Truth cannot be invented.

*****

The truth about humans is not human.

*****

The truth prosecutes.

*****

Are we more frequently eager to believe lies than we are eager to believe the truth?

*****

Truth can destroy a lie where a lie can conceal the truth yet not destroy it.

U

UNDERSTANDING

One need not understand to listen.

*****

Human communication is based more on how we misunderstand each other than on understanding. Animals rarely, if ever, misunderstand each other. So who is more intelligent?

*****

Most people think being misunderstood is a result of the other persons misunderstanding rather than their own.

*****

There can be no real understanding of why marriage ends, why athletes lose strength, why government and religious policies fail, without understanding the nature of the intervals in the law of seven.

*****

It is better to understand the process of understanding rather than the thing to be understood.

*****

There can be no complete understanding on any subject until a study of that subject has passed the second interval of the law of seven.

*****

We are more defensive about what we do not understand than about what we do understand.

*****

Understanding by definition means that we have only one antenna up instead of twenty, thirty or a hundred.

*****

We must first understand by the definition of logic that understanding by perception is greater than understanding by the definition of logic.

UNIVERSE

All knowledge of the universe, to be correct, must include the self-knowledge of man.

*****

Man and the universe he sees are made of the same generation of species and events.

*****

Why don't we smell or hear the universe? Or why do we see it as a universe rather than as the skeleton of some beast, a grave, an egg or a mistake.

*****

V

VALUE

The true value of a person is measured by that person's abiiity to hold his attention on himself in the present. It is not measured by beauty, wealth, talent, fame, goodness, influence, family heritage or devotion. Before the present all people are beggars.

*****

Faith, art, science, religion cannot be placed above enlightenment—above the effort to be in the present which leads to enlightenment. They can be added to enlightenment but they cannot stand above it. This is the problem—our categories of value are improperly set.

*****

Good and evil cannot be measured by a man's desire for well being.

*****

The inherent evolutionary value of a thing determines its worth.

*****

The concept of name recognition as a means of measuring the value of a person, product or event is a two dimensional concept.

VELOCITY

The greater the velocity the greater the absence of identity of form.

*****

W

WATER

A deep pool of calm water gives us a view of the second and third dimensions simultaneously, as we can see reflection off its two-dimensional surface while looking into its three dimensional depth. An awareness of more than one dimension at a time is difficult for us to achieve.

*****

WISDOM

There is no doubt that the gods are wiser than we; yet we would be more foolish than we are, not to doubt them.

*****

No man is so wise that he cannot gain more wisdom.

*****

Those who can bare the truth would be wise.

*****

Wisdom is born out of connected moments of understanding, not out of accumulated reactions. This being so, aging can not guarantee the arrival of wisdom.

*****

How much of a man's wisdom is directed toward supporting his faults?

*****

He is a wise man who cultivates the friendship and love of women wiser than he.

*****

Seeing that another man's wisdom and goodness is greater than mine does not make me less wise or less good.

*****

It is unwise to approach a question as if there were only one answer.

*****

An interpreter of events is not so wise as an observer of events.

*****

Wisdom is always a question of how impersonally we can see ourselves without losing the natural warmth of our human nature.

*****

Faith and belief are less than wisdom.

*****

How wise is the man who achieves self-importance by assuming others are less important than he?

*****

How many there are with very little wisdom who speak as through they are wise because they have a little bit of power.

*****

Prepare to meet a man of wisdom by becoming a man of wisdom.

*****

WOMEN

Women have been given a minor role in the making and administering of religion, not because they are less worthy, but because men instinctively fear that the greater perceptivity of women would expose the illusion of masculine superiority which binds followers to religious code.

*****

A great woman is greater than a great man.

*****

A man will serve his own needs first, whereas a woman will often serve others first.

*****

It is not just the male animal but society as a whole that makes the mistake of seeing women as second-class citizens.

*****

Women are not loved enough.

*****

Woman's greater need for human closeness comes from her ability to carry a human being within her womb.

*****

A man who has not had an intimate relationship with a women has not yet become a man.

*****

At one end of the scale women are degraded by the macho chauvinist and at the other end they are mocked by the synthetic femininity of the reprobate homosexual. Mankind is still at a great distance from equality among equals.

*****

No matter how much a man loves a women he cannot claim to understand her until he has developed in himself a level of emotional perception which is equal to hers.

*****

The female can be seen as the superior species when the inherent perceptivity of the female psyche is compare to that of the male psyche. For example, at a typical business dinner the wives of the men will notice many emotional details about the relationships between those at the dinner, where the men will notice little more than the proportions of the women and if a deal can be made. The most perceptive of the four lower brains is the emotion brain, thus the female, in being centred in the emotional brain, will tend to be emotionally more perceptive than the male. Greater emotional perception is absolutely necessary for the development of the soul. Men, in general, have less of this kind of perception and are therefore less capable as a species of evolving the overall race of mankind. Once this truth has been recognized and women are better understood, the use of their greater perceptivity will help to evolve the species. Women are, quite simply, better dedigned to give birth than men are. Yet it is the men who are trying to give birth to our species and the are not doing a good job.

*****

WORSHIP

Those who worship God and those who worship Satan do so for the same reasons. Both wish to be protected, to have power over their enemies, to survive death, to right the wrongs done to them, to gain a source of hope.

*****

ADDITIONAL THOUGHTS

The time taken to criticize the faults of others is the best time to criticize
our own faults.

*****

The only guarantee of success is success itself.

*****

An angel is not without cunning.

*****

We do not choose to be weak.

*****

Life on earth may be more like the life that goes on inside our stomachs
than like the life we see before our eyes.

*****

It is easier to explain how I came here than to describe what I saw when
I arrived.

*****

One by-product of a consumer society is that the measure of a man's
worth is seen as being equal to his commercial value.

*****

A mistake is not so often wrong as it is thought wrong.

*****

The truth in what I have said is not in my saying it.

*****

Self-examination stops with the word bored.

*****

The sun does not have a shadow.

*****

Many big questions have little answers.

*****

The motives for honesty are not so much in question as the motives for dishonesty.

*****

Virtues do not oppose each other, men do, and all claim opposition is virtuous.

*****

We are unintelligent when we fail to question, not when we fail to have answers.

*****

Less creative people get an identity out of what they create.

*****

We act mostly in accordance with what is expected of us rather than from what we expect of ourselves.

*****

The gliding of a bird is almost without waste.

*****

I can speak and you can listen, but it is better for me to write it down and for you to hear it in your own voice.

*****

Light is a waste product of the sun.

*****

You want me to answer your questions in a way that you understand, rather than to give you a new understanding.

*****

There is no doubt that many people want new ideas. The problem is all the old ideas which refuse to digest out of the system.

*****

What makes it difficult makes it possible.

*****

The hope of enlightenment is man's greatest hope. While having this hope, he is most weak. No greater crime can be committed than abuse of this hope.

*****

Thoughts and ideas migrate through time and space just as birds migrate here.

*****

People only say thank you for what they are given, not for what they take.

*****

While seeing from inside one's self the skull seems heavy, the arms and legs are way out there and nobody appears to notice you.

*****

She has plans for herself, we can see, because she has plans for other people.

*****

There can be no greatness without freedom.

*****

Freedom from gravity underlies our fascination with fire, bombs, orgasms, and explosions of all kinds.

*****

Moths feed on the light they pursue.

*****

He loses pride who is too proud.

*****

Believe nothing, trust no one.

*****

Opposing ignorance is not godlessness.

*****

But why should I come to know man so well, for soon time shall do away with us. Isn't it better that I come to know time?

*****

More than knowing, ours is a question of keeping ourselves from thinking that we know.

*****

You are welcome to find fault with me but not without my seeing your faults.

*****

Observation combined with patience yields contemplation.

*****

A thought can outlast the sun.

*****

Fame would be less popular if people were more interested in themselves, than they are in having others interested in them.

*****

When we were young we doubted age, now we doubt our youth.

*****

It is easier to choose between a devil and an angel, than between two angels or two devils.

*****

What gave a particle of light the courage to come into existence?

*****

That we do not know is obvious, how much we do not know is the question.

*****

I know the world
I've sucked her milkless breast
I've vomited
from the saints
And survived myself.

*****

It is not so much an interest in winning, as one of not losing.

*****

Naturally we are only in favour of what benefits us.

*****

Great entertainers are more popular than great teachers, because it is easier to be entertained than it is to learn.

*****

The only people who do not have contradictions are those who cannot see the contradictions that they have.

*****

With the rising of each sun, men bubble up from their sleep like molecules of water in a pot on a hot stove. And is there much difference between the men and the molecules?

*****

The life of silence intrigues me more than all the festivals of kings.

*****

It is more difficult to respect someone when we do not understand him.

*****

Powerful men make themselves needed more than wanted.

*****

All men are free to make mistakes, but few are free enough to rise above them.

*****

Reserve the right to think well of yourself.

*****

Is he made a criminal who sees a crime?

*****

Few men have more cunning than their own weaknesses.

*****

That a man is followed does not make him a leader.

*****

The absence of the soul cannot be felt until after the soul has been created.

*****

Those who speak with successive profundities are the least profound.

*****

A certain man will pause while an uncertain man will hesitate.

*****

Spirit is not a performance.

*****

Corruption has very limited creative possibilities.

*****

How convenient it is for us to assume that what we do not like about someone is a result of that person's weaknesses and faults.

*****

We are given no choice but to protect ourselves when we meet someone who automatically assumes himself to be superior to us.

*****

Little men with little power make the same mistakes as big men with big power.

*****

There is a great difference between a thinking person and an educated one.

*****

No man is as perfect as a good idea.

*****

To listen is one of man's greatest expressions of respect.

*****

Know the difference between concern and manipulation.

*****

As we view bugs, so are we viewed by the earth, planets and the sun.

*****

The pause of pondering dominates.

*****

When Human Rights are in question—man as a human being is in question.

*****

Assuming that they have no ignorance, ignorant people speak about knowledge as though there is nothing beyond what they know.

*****

There is no other means of acquiring strength than through weakness.

*****

They are not wrong, but they do not know why they are right.

*****

Flies have no fences

*****

I would trust more frequently the wisdom of a prostitute than that of a politician.

*****

Innocence feeds the world.

*****

You don't have something unless you have something to give.

*****

A powerful man will ask the advice of a weak man to prove to himself that he has no need of advice.

*****

There is a right time to learn from one's mistakes.

*****

Love learning and love will never leave you.

*****

Great men need not be known, yet the knowledge of great men must be.

*****

I have drawn a straight line ;with a circular motion.

*****

Reasons for questioning are different from reasons for answering.

*****

Intimacy is not a sin.

*****

The chest is the most innocent part of the body.

*****

I wonder, would aliens find we humans and our homes more impressive at night or in the daytime.

*****

We can not have a war without youth.

*****

One of the worst things about many problems is thinking that we have them.

*****

I am not so often the wise man that I wish to be as I am the man I am wishing to be wise.

*****

A man with real power appears powerless.

*****

Much of respect is a veiled form of fear. Respect without fear is rare.

*****

An ear one can speak to. To a mouth one can not speak.

*****

ONE NEED NOT BE IN A FLOCK TO FLY

*****